W9-CGW-454

What We've Learned So Far

WHAT WE'VE LEARNED SO FAR

Thoughts on Turning 50
from
Today's Favorite
Christian Women Leaders

LUCINDA SECREST MCDOWELL

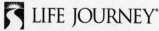

LIFE JOURNEY

Bringing Home the Message for Life

COOK COMMUNICATIONS MINISTRIES
Colorado Springs, Colorado • Paris, Ontario
KINGSWAY COMMUNICATIONS LTD.
Eastbourne, England

Life Journey® is an imprint of
Cook Communications Ministries, Colorado Springs, CO 80918
Cook Communications, Paris, Ontario
Kingsway Communications, Eastbourne, England

WHAT WE'VE LEARNED SO FAR
© 2004 by Lucinda Secrest McDowell

Published in association with the literary agency of Alive Communications, 7680 Goddard St., STE. 200, Colorado Springs, CO 80920.

Printed in the United States of America

Cover Design: Marks & Whetstone
Cover Photos: Royalty Free/Photodisk

ISBN 0-7394-6238-5

For my daughters
Fiona Johanna Yvonne McDowell
and
Margaret Sarah Secrest McDowell

May both of you always know the
grit, grace, and glory
of being a woman who loves and serves God.
And may you embrace these
important truths earlier than I did!

Contents

Acknowledgments

My heart is full of gratitude for each of you women who so graciously contributed your story for this book. Thank you, dear sisters, for being so real and so encouraging.

Special thanks to my best friend and prayer partner, Maggie Rowe, and to all my praying AWSA cheerleaders who keep me going every day.

I also want to say a huge thanks to my precious family—Mike, Justin, Tim, Fiona, and Maggie—for their love and grace to me during this past year and for celebrating with me every day this wonderful gift of Life.

Words of appreciation also go to my literary agent, Chip MacGregor of Alive Communications, and my Cook Communications editor, Mary McNeil, for their wonderful partnership in this book project.

Most of all, thank You, dear Lord, for Your mercies which are new every morning. Great is Your faithfulness.

Introduction

[I] will celebrate your abundant goodness
and joyfully sing of your righteousness.

Psalm 145:7

It will happen to four million people this year in the United States, and today it happened to *me!*

I turned fifty years old—a milestone most baby boomers think will never come.

No matter how we look at it, turning fifty is a Big Deal.

And it should be. After all, those of us who have reached that venerable age have survived half a century. We have experienced many different seasons of life and have somehow managed to dress accordingly for each one. We have *been* babies and *had* babies, and now are witnessing *our babies having babies.* Our generation of women will always be known as the one that paved the way for women to succeed in every arena of life. We have *become* those professional women that little girls now want to grow up to be (even though all we knew about growing up to be when we were little girls were mamas, teachers, nurses, or secretaries).

And we are much wiser for all this living. Because we have discovered that it is *during the journey of life* that we develop wisdom and sensitivity and grace and understanding and compassion and generosity and humility. Oh yes, we may have had firmer bodies and sharper minds when we were twenty, but we didn't know all that much about ourselves, other people, the world, and God.

It took some fits and starts to get to where we are now. It took

11

achievement tempered by failure. It took both joy and sorrow, gain and loss. But now we have evolved, and some of us have even reinvented ourselves. Who we are now looks nothing like the dreams we had when we were young. But that's only because we didn't even know enough then to dream this big.

Turning fifty can be a time of discovery that there is still so much more in life: more of God and more of celebration and more of people who touch us forever. Most of all, it should be an occasion to celebrate with gratitude the experiences and people that have shaped us and left their marks on us.

Do you celebrate the gift of life each day? My father's motto has always been "It's a great day to be alive!" Do you believe that? It would be easy to look around at our circumstances and the uncertainty of today's world and throw our hands up in despair. But, as King David proclaimed in Psalm 145:7, we can celebrate God and His unchanging character of love and faithfulness to us, and that in spite of many difficulties without and within.

Such a milestone as my fiftieth birthday certainly has me reflecting on the passage of time since my own birth year:

Back in 1953, Dwight D. Eisenhower was President of the United States, and during his campaign for election many people wore buttons stating, "I Like Ike." When he visited my hometown of Thomasville, Georgia, my grandfather took him golfing.

Back in 1953, the hottest new songs were "How Much Is That Doggie in the Window?" and "Your Cheatin' Heart."

Back in 1953, Elizabeth was crowned Queen of England at age twenty-seven, and Sir Edmund Hillary, age thirty-four, became the first man to reach the peak of Mount Everest, an achievement he presented as his "coronation gift" to her.

Back in 1953, the two most popular non-fiction books were Norman Vincent Peale's *The Power of Positive Thinking* and Catherine Marshall's *A Man Called Peter*. Most moviegoers went to see *The Robe* and *From Here to Eternity*.

I am amazed at the radical changes in culture and worldview since then, and not always for the best. But the good news is that God has not changed, and by His grace His people continue to grow in knowledge, wisdom, and faith.

So, what have I learned so far? I have condensed it into these Seven Most Important Truths:

1. Who I Am Is More Important Than What I Do
2. God Is in Control
3. Relationships Are to Be Celebrated
4. Freedom Is Found in Simplicity
5. Pain Either Destroys or Transforms
6. Life Is Full of Surprises
7. Perseverance Pays Off

Then I thought of fifty of my friends and contemporaries, authors and speakers who are honest and faith-filled and eager to share the wisdom of their lives. I am so grateful that each woman was happy to be part of a project designed to convey the positive aspects of this time of life. Together we have fleshed out with transparency and vulnerability these important truths that now govern who we are and what we do with each new day we are given.

As you read these stories, it is our desire that you laugh, cry, relate, and be moved to pray for strength and perseverance to live to the fullest the life God has for you today. May you rejoice in your years and dedicate whatever time is left of them to pursuing only the most important things. Time is far too limited to waste. And it is never too late to write the story of the rest of your life.

Ours is a God of a thousand new beginnings.

Lucinda Secrest McDowell
Gracehaven
Wethersfield, Connecticut
May 23, 2003

TRUTH ONE:

Who I Am Is More Important Than What I Do

"Striving No More"

BY LUCINDA SECREST MCDOWELL

I am so thankful to live in a family who keeps me honest. In fact, my eldest son, who was born with mental retardation, can always be counted on to "tell it like it is." This is probably a good thing because: (1) I am not tempted to live a secret life, since all the juicy details would inevitably come out; and, (2) Justin, with his total lack of guile, willingly offers me a daily critique of all my words and actions (and, only rarely, my appearance).

Therefore, any preconceived notions I may have had in my twenties, thirties, or even forties about succeeding in life due to my achievements or credentials have summarily been discarded in favor of just *being me*.

My first lesson in this particular "free to be me" characteristic came in my early thirties when I entered into two blissful states simultaneously—marriage and motherhood. Now, I know the *normal* way is to get used to being married first, then slowly add children; but I guess God took one look at me and decided that since I wasn't getting any younger, I may as well get started on my family. So I fell in love with a widower and eventually went through the court system to adopt his three children.

Needless to say, after a move from San Francisco to Seattle I discovered that I *did not* know how to do everything I was doing, and everything I *did* know how to do was only a distant memory in a faraway world. Though delighted to embrace this new season of at-home motherhood, I was definitely on a high learning curve. The only thing in my life that hadn't changed was God. But He had definitely accompanied me and was intent on setting me free from my tendency to find meaning in activity.

Still, it was a challenging time of reevaluating my own sense of identity. I had worked hard for my professional achievements, but I wasn't really sure where *they* ended and *I* began. Who was I now that my audience was three little ones rather than a congregation of a thousand? And writing grocery lists wasn't exactly keeping me in tune with the publishing world. But God was clearly helping me to understand grace—His great gift of love for me that I don't deserve and can never earn, no matter how much I may "accomplish" for Him.

And a little child led the way.

It was a typical rainy Seattle day when I turned to my son while helping him with a puzzle, "Justin, what do you want to be when you grow up?"

He quickly answered, "A professional basketball player" and turned the tables.

"Mom, when you were my age, what did *you* want to be?"

Oh, I was ready. In fifth grade I had read a biography of Madame Marie Curie, and even though I knew no female doctors at the time, my hopes had been high. "Justin, when I was nine years old I wanted more than anything to grow up to be a doctor."

To which he immediately replied in his innocent and candid way, "And look what you became—just a regular old lady."

Inside I cringed and wanted to cry out defensively, "Excuse me, a regular old lady? I'll have you know that I have a master's degree and have published articles and I traveled around the world twice before I was thirty and …"

But of course, I didn't.

Which was a good thing since none of that would have impressed him at all. What he most wanted and needed from me *was* that I be just a "regular old lady"—the one who was always there when his bus dropped him off from school, who cheered for him in Special Olympics, made oatmeal cookies, and read with him each evening.

In this *kairos* moment God showed me how unimportant my accumulated credentials were for where He had placed me and what He had given me to do. By saying yes to motherhood, I inevitably had to say no to some other really tempting opportunities. After some overachievement and burnout I eventually realized that I didn't need to strive to earn my new family's love any more than I did to earn God's love. Carefully, slowly, I began to feel joy in the priority of nurturing my children and supporting my husband through seasons of productivity as well as seasons when only one thing was checked off my to-do list at the end of the day.

It was a new understanding of God's grace that gave me freedom to rest in who I am, a person with both strengths and limitations. And I was cheered on by the apostle Paul's example: "My ego is no longer central. It is no longer important that I appear righteous before you or have your good opinion, and I am no longer driven to impress God. Christ lives in me. The life you see me living is not 'mine,' but it is lived by faith in the Son of God, who loved me and gave himself for me. I am not going to go back on that. … I refuse to do that, to repudiate God's grace" (Gal. 2:20–21 MSG).

Justin is a grown man now, but his astute questions and comments still keep me focused on what's most important. In my first fifty years there have been some pretty exciting open doors that I have walked through and some pretty devastating ones which have threatened to topple me as they slammed shut in my face. But through it all I have managed to cling to the real me. Raising two sons and two daughters has humbled me in ways I never imagined and clarified the truth that real time, generosity, a gentle tone of voice, and availability are a far greater legacy than job titles, stock options, book contracts, and the applause of thousands.

Sometimes we get a taste of both the mundane and the glamorous in this life. But I am delighted to join the ranks of mid-lifers who echo the truth, "Middle age is that point when you realize that all of life is a gift." Released from being a POW (prisoner of works), I am now content to be just me—a person who is occasionally a public success but sometimes a private failure. God loves me, and His grace is there for me, so that whatever comes my way, I can take it all.

Lucinda Secrest McDowell, M.T.S. (Connecticut) presents "Encouraging Words that Transform" through her international conference speaking and writing. A graduate of Gordon-Conwell Seminary, she is the author of five books including *Quilts from Heaven, Women's Spiritual Passages,* and *Amazed by Grace.* www.EncouragingWords.net

"Feet First"

BY GRACIE MALONE

When the sun peeked over the horizon one spring morning, I groaned, turned my back to the window, and covered my head with a pillow. Unfortunately, it failed to muffle the buzz of the alarm clock that sounded a few minutes later. *Aaarrrghh!* I hit the snooze button. If only I had a switch to turn off the thoughts that began to trek through my befuddled brain.

Tonight I'll be speaking at a women's ministry dinner at a nearby church. I need to go over my notes, and, just in case the gals at the dinner might be interested in what I've written, I need to load a few boxes of books into the back of my SUV. It's time for me to get going.

I threw back the covers and headed toward the kitchen where the coffee was already perking. (Thanks to its own unique "alarm" clock, it gets started before I do.) After two sips of the flavorful brew, I picked up the phone and called the Terrace Day Spa. "I have such a busy day planned, that, well … I need to come in for a pedicure."

Now, I know what you are thinking. *If you're pressed for time, why add to an overcrowded schedule? If you're stressed, why not attend a prayer retreat instead of making an appointment at a day spa?* So, I am going to tell you straight out something that has taken me fifty years to learn: Being kind to myself—physically—is important, maybe even *equally important,* to nurturing my spiritual self. After all, if I am out of sorts, tired, or distracted, then my spiritual condition is ... well ... not worth the paper my message is written on. On the other hand, once my physical problems are solved, my spirit soars higher than a kite on a windy March afternoon.

Before you decide that I am shallow, let me remind you that God created the human body—and He created it *first.* Spiritual life came second. The physical and spiritual parts of our selves are so closely intertwined that we cannot neglect one without hurting the other. For as long as we live on planet earth, we will have to care for our bodies as well as our spirits, and that includes dealing with physical limitations, the effects of aging, and the pain of certain afflictions like arthritis and swollen bunions.

To one person, caring for the body may mean taking a well-deserved nap, relaxing with a good book, or going for a long walk along a country road. For someone else, it may be sitting down to a nutritious meal, kicking back in a comfy chair, settling on a porch swing, or taking a long soak in the bathtub. For me, it means putting my feet first. Okay, I will admit that taking these puppies to a day spa might be considered a bit extravagant, but at least I came to enjoy this luxury after grasping a few spiritual insights.

A few years ago, after teaching the last session of a Bible study series, one of the gals in the group presented me a gift. Extending a package and card my direction, she grinned mischievously and said, "Open the box first."

I unwrapped a cute little pair of bright-pink, feather-enhanced, high-heeled shoes, sized to fit a preschool girl. *Hummm,* I thought, *my granddaughters will enjoy these when they play "dress-up."* I tore open the card and read the words, "How beautiful are the feet of those who bring good news!" (Rom. 10:15). I brushed away a tear as I thought about how dear this group of women had become. But my wacky sense of humor wouldn't allow me to bob about in deep waters too long. I covered a silly grin with my hand as I thought, *Beautiful is not the adjective I would use to describe my callused tootsies.* Then I noticed a gift certificate tucked inside the card. It was for a pedicure. I thanked the group for their thoughtfulness and sat down, wondering if I would ever have the nerve to redeem that coupon.

At home, I placed the shoes on my desk where they stayed for several months, a reminder of the love expressed by my friends. Occasionally I thought about the gift certificate and wondered what a pedicure felt like. I have to admit the idea intrigued me, but it seemed so contrary to what Jesus would do. He would be the One doing the washing, wouldn't He? I just couldn't imagine allowing somebody to wash my feet and polish my toenails.

Then one day I re-read a familiar story about Jesus and His disciples. They had gathered for the Passover Feast. After the meal, Jesus "poured water into a basin and began to wash his disciples' feet" (John 13:5). Peter probably expressed the feelings of the whole group when he said, "Lord, are you going to wash my feet? … never …" (vv. 6, 8). I am sure I would have felt that same way. But then as I pondered the verses, I noticed something I hadn't seen before. Jesus did this to show His disciples "the full extent of his love" (v. 1). To refuse Jesus' act of devotion would have been to refuse His everlasting love. Peter must have realized this fact, for he quickly, willingly, submitted to the footwashing.

I began to wonder if my reluctance to cash in on the love gift from my friends really had anything to do with my desire to be like Jesus? Or was it more a matter of resisting the grace of God—that special grace that gregarious people like me (or like Peter) need in order to be on the receiving end of someone else's gift of service?

The very next day I made an appointment for a footwashing. It was the first of several. Today, whenever I feel my stress level rising, or whenever the pressure to perform pushes me out of my comfort zone, I call the spa. I love relaxing in the attendant's vibrating chair, feeling the warm swirling water as it washes my feet. As she rubs walnut granule exfoliating cream into my calluses and massages my tired legs and ankles with warm oil, I feel totally rejuvenated and ready to face whatever might come my way. Besides all that, I think my feet with their brightly colored nails look absolutely beautiful.

Gracie Malone (Texas) is a wife, mother, grandmother, Bible study teacher, mentor of women, and frequent speaker at conferences and retreats. Her latest books are *Off My Rocker!, Sunshine for Grandmas,* and *Still Making Waves.* www.GracieMalone.com

"What I'm Made For"

BY KAREN MAINS

One of the greatest terrors in my life is double-bookings, promising to be in two places at the same time. I regularly go over my travel calendar with a fine-tooth comb, cross-reference it against my at-home planning calendar, then check everything with my personal Day Runner and, finally, against David's three-year calendar with the month-at-a-glance pages. Very infrequently, embarrassing glitches do happen. ...

This particular year I had agreed to act as chairperson for my home church's Women's Retreat on the same weekend I had accepted a speaking engagement in the Baltimore area. After some self-recrimination, I decided to look on this latest faux pas as a test of my administrative capacities. So I prepared decorations and details, divided the Retreat responsibilities according to time/events and chose a woman leader for each section, then left the event in capable hands and drove to the airport.

Only after being ensconced in my motel room in Baltimore did I realize that I was exhausted.

I crawl into bed, aware finally that fatigue is spreading to the very marrow of my bones; I am so weary my body aches if I roll over. I remind myself that one of the reasons I took on the responsibilities for the Women's Retreat was because I so often fly into conferences, do my thing, reap the harvest of other women's hard behind-the-scenes labor, and fly out, trailing their glory behind me.

Public living is dangerous in that the temptation to gather too much credit unto oneself is indigenous to success. There is nothing more leveling than the reality of doing the thankless grunt work. However, I never intended doing both at the same time. I turn out the light; my feet are cramping. I get up, swallow some calcium capsules, crawl groaning back to bed. I sleep fitfully, exhaustion deep-creasing my muscles, my bones lie heavy, as though weighted by leg irons.

The next day I know I am in physical trouble. Having spoken once, and while the women are in workshops, I am led to the youth pastor's office where there is quiet, a couch, and a clock on the wall by which I can monitor a catnap. I am so tired I can hardly lift my knees to climb the stairs. I wonder: *How can I minister to these women when I can't even pray for them?*

In the middle of my third speech, the last, that inward word comes to me as distinctly as though I had heard it out loud: *You are made for the giving and the receiving of love.* Emphasis is on the last half of the statement. *The receiving of love.*

Suddenly I see the women who are sitting before me. I see love in their eyes as they look up at me. I have spent years protecting myself, wrapping my heart with plastic and spraying it with Teflon so that I wouldn't succumb to the allure of celebrityitis. Suddenly, tired and weary and holding to the podium for the strength to go on—no longer the competent wonder-woman-administrative-genius—I understand as I never have before that there is a mutual exchange that must occur in ministry. These women have as much to give me as I have to give them.

Continuing with my outline, my voice functions from habit, but my mind is actually repeating to myself the inner words I have heard. I open myself to these people sitting at my feet; they are hungry for spiritual reality, longing for practical truth, and at this moment they are receiving it from my shaking hand. Their wave of favor embraces me—these women who because of my fatigue are being so inadequately taught—and I consciously let love into my aching body.

I am made for the giving of love. I am made for the receiving of love.

I have considered this Maryland meeting a glitch on my schedule, proof of my need for still-to-be-improved-upon efficiency. Now I begin to consider that perhaps I haven't double-booked myself; perhaps it is God who has designed this dysfunction. Perhaps it is He who has something to teach me, something profound I need to hear.

When I am functioning efficiently, inner reminders are often lost in the middle of lists, plans, time lines, and agendas. It's when the microchip in my brain glitches that instruction comes. How often, like the apostle Paul, I kick against these goads, privately fuming at my own inabilities. But it is in the pauses that I am forced to reconsider. It is in the bad moments of my life that I must choose to learn the opportunity that hides at its deepest center. When my inadequacies rise, rebelling against my carefully constructed external persona then—then—God can get my attention.

Karen Mains (Illinois) serves as co-director with her husband, David, of Mainstay Ministries. An award-winning author, her most recent book is *The God Hunt.* Karen also directs Hungry Souls, a ministry for self-direction and spiritual growth through peer mentoring. www.HungrySouls.org

"Becoming the Best Possible You"

BY LESLIE VERNICK

Have you ever wondered if you're becoming the worst possible version of yourself?"

I have. This question from the movie *You've Got Mail*, hit me like a bolt of lightning when I heard it. I began to wonder what would the best possible version of myself look like? Not just on the outside where others see me, but on the inside, where the real me lives.

As God's children we are his image bearers and He tells us that as we mature, we are to look more and more like Him. Dietrich Bonhoeffer, a Lutheran pastor martyred under Hitler during World War II, said in his classic book, *The Cost of Discipleship*, "Every man bears an image. Either man models himself on the god of his own invention, or the true living God molds the human form into His image. There must be a complete transformation, a 'metamorphosis' if man is to be restored to the image of God." The good news of the gospel is that God doesn't just redeem us; He also restores us.

As human beings we, too, have lost our God-given beauty. We have been damaged and tarnished through sin; both our own sin as well as the sin of others against us. When God redeems us, He doesn't just cleanse us from our impurities. That is only the beginning, but not the end. He then begins the process of restoring us so that we might better reflect His image and Christ's nature in our human body (see 2 Cor. 4:10). In this process, God's plan isn't to change us into another person. He wants to transform us so that we become the best possible version of ourselves, the version He originally created us to be—like Jesus.

Perhaps one of the reasons that many of us find ourselves still stuck in repetitive patterns of immaturity and sin is that although we have heard these truths, we have never really applied them to the details of our everyday lives. God demonstrated this to me through my daughter Amanda.

Over the past thirteen years Amanda has taken piano lessons. I have sat in on her weekly sessions and I have learned more about notes, timing, piano theory, composition, and composers than I ever knew before. I could even teach beginning piano students some of the basics. Yet, I cannot play the piano like Amanda. Why not? Because I never took any of the things that I learned each week and put them into practice. I know them in my head; I just don't know how to do them with my fingers.

Many Christians sit in church every week, attend Bible study, have devotions, and still find ourselves looking more like ourselves than like Jesus. We feel frustrated in our spiritual life and often say things like, "I know that in my head, I just don't know how to live it in my heart." Perhaps one reason that we do not experience more reality to our spiritual life is because we have not fully surrendered to God our old ways of thinking and doing things, nor have we applied what He is showing and teaching us to our daily lives. If we did, then we would be growing, changing, and becoming more what He intended for us to become.

This experience with my daughter illustrated for me an

important aspect of my spiritual growth. Over those thirteen years of piano lessons, there were times that I sat down and tried to play the piano, but I was never consistent. Amanda became a great pianist because she faithfully practiced what her piano teacher taught her each week. I only listened.

Just as I occasionally tried to play the piano I realized that for a long time in my Christian life, I sporadically tried to be more like Jesus. I tried to be more patient, more loving, more of the person God wanted me to be. Sometimes I tried harder than others, but ultimately I always failed. In my frustration, God revealed that He never tells us to try to be more like Him. Instead, He tells us to train. The apostle Paul says, "Train yourself to be godly" (1 Tim. 4:7), and Jesus taught, "A student is not above his teacher, but everyone who is fully trained will be like his teacher" (Luke 6:40). We don't learn God's ways by trying, but we can learn them through training.

Amanda learned to play the piano by listening to her teacher's instructions and daily putting them into practice. Sometimes, when it became difficult, Amanda was tempted to give up the piano, but she persevered and trained to develop her talent as a musician. Sometimes I, too, have been tempted to give up when training in Christ's school of holiness. Dying to my old ways and learning how to live and love and think like Christ isn't easy. Yet the writer of Hebrews encourages us to stick with it by reminding us that, "no discipline seems pleasant at the time, but painful. Later on, however, it produces a harvest of righteousness and peace for those who have been trained by it" (Heb. 12:11).

Our lives are meant for a far greater purpose than just pleasing or satisfying ourselves. We have an opportunity to live a life that matters for all of eternity. God desires to restore His nature and His image in us, but only if we are willing students, yielding ourselves daily to Him.

Do you want to become the best possible version of yourself? Stop trying and start training.

Leslie Vernick (Pennsylvania), a licensed clinical social worker, speaker, and author, has a heart for people and a passion for God. She is the author of three books and many articles. www.LeslieVernick.com

"Turning Things Around"

BY ANNE WHEELER-WADDELL

I take myself far too seriously. But God puts up with me anyway. In fact, even after twenty-two years of seeking to live with God at the center of my life, I might be, just a little, almost, maybe, realizing that God not only *puts up* with me, He actually *celebrates* me.

I have been sincerely saddened when I hear stories of women who, after years of sublimating their true selves because of insecure spouses or the demands of family, finally break out to become who they truly are. The sadness I feel when I hear such stories is because of the lost years and often the broken families involved. It has made me more aware of the grace I have known, never having felt held back or hindered. I answered God's call to ministry, and the doors to ordination flew open at every step.

My dream of returning to East Africa was answered in 1982, and I began what has been a nineteen-year career in cross-cultural ministry. Answering a long and quietly held desire, God brought John into my life during an extended leave from Kenya. We were married, and I, at age thirty-nine, had to laugh to think how long it apparently had taken for God to prepare me for this calling. But what an incredible gift it is to share life and ministry with a man who loves God and has given his life to following Christ—one who celebrates my gifts and abilities as well as his own. Truly "the lines have fallen to me in pleasant places" (Ps. 16:6 NASB).

So, when John and I both began to feel restless after several years in Kenya and answered what we believed to be God's call to rural Ethiopia, we walked through another open door. We had gone to help start a Bible school in a part of Ethiopia where the church was (and continues to be) experiencing tremendous growth. We would be in on the ground floor, we thought, teaching and training those already out there leading congregations. And, we envisioned, we would be helping train and prepare Ethiopian teachers as together we created a formative atmosphere for theological training and shaped an appropriate curriculum.

Well, the long and short of it is, after a year in the capital struggling to get a handle on the Amharic language, we were to confront a greater disappointment when we discovered that the building of the school and our house had ground to a halt. But our first week out, we discovered people who were so eager for teaching that we were prevailed upon to stay for eight nights. Yet even though we tried to get out in the parishes to teach, the physical demands became too much. After a bout of shigella cut short this week, our Ethiopian colleague, perhaps discouraged by our physical frailty, did not plan any more parish visits. Other attempts at teaching venues brought one or two opportunities, but language difficulties meant that these, too, were short-lived.

So, I found myself in our small nine-hundred-square-foot home with nothing life-giving to do. I spent months in that small house crying out to a silent God. "Why did You bring us here? Why did You bring me here to do nothing? What if the Bible school never gets built? How long do we wait? Who am I, Lord? If I am not preaching and teaching, if I am not using my gifts, who am I?" I cried out to God and protested to my husband, "I told you from the beginning that I'm not a housewife. You didn't marry me to be a housewife and a cook. That's not who I am. I'm dying here." Those were painful, silent months (except for my groanings), times full of self-questioning and great self-doubt.

Just as our term was coming to a close and we were leaving, the Bible school facility was completed, school opened, and we had the opportunity to teach in the Bible school during a two-week course for evangelists. It has taken the better part of a year of prayer and process to realize that God always knows what is happening and why.

The day before we left Addis Ababa, our neighbor from down south came to see us. He was in the capital for an accounting course. Between my broken Amharic and his less broken English we spent several hours visiting, talking about home, back down south. Then he said to me something like, "Qes Hannah, I know we had many difficulties in the Synod, and there were many problems, but I hope this has been a good experience for you." Feeling quite honest, I replied to my friend, "It has been very difficult and disappointing. I am a teacher. I love to teach the Bible. We came here to build people, but for three years we mainly built buildings." My friend was quiet, and then in broken English he replied, "Oh, but the fact that you and Qes John came, and you stayed even when it was difficult, *that* has been a teaching for us."

I could have cried and hugged him, had it been culturally appropriate. Whether or not he was being very kind and saying what he thought I wanted to hear, I heard God speaking through him, and I have lived with that quiet truth for a year now.

Our culture teaches us to *do*, to *produce*, and to have something to *show* for it all. There is great value in our doing both for ourselves and for those blessed to receive what we have offered. While pastoring and teaching involve doing many good and needful things, I have long believed that ministry grows out of *being*. Too often, however, the expectations of *doing* crowd out the space or expectation we have of ourselves for *being*. My senses of self-worth and contribution have been too much wrapped up in the positive feedback I receive from teaching a lesson or preaching a sermon. If I am not doing these things, what I am really contributing? I know how to *do*. It is frightening just to *be*. I can make things happen by doing. But being is something I have to wait for. It takes great patience and a greater grace.

But maybe, after all these years, I am beginning to realize what I have said I believe: "For by grace you have been saved through faith, and this is not your own doing; it is the gift of God—not the result of works, so that no one may boast. For we are what he has made us, created in Christ Jesus for good works, which God prepared beforehand to be our way of life" (Eph. 2:8–10 NRSV).

It has taken half a century, but maybe I am just beginning to live in that greater grace that is not my own doing. Thanks be to God!

Anne Wheeler-Waddell (Ethiopia) is an ordained Presbyterian minister and has been a pastor/educator mission co-worker in Kenya and Ethiopia. Recently her ministry has included pastoral care and spiritual encouragement with cross-cultural mission personnel. The ocean, mountains, and walks with her husband John nourish her soul.

"Talking to Strangers"

BY DEB HAGGERTY

Once upon a time I was very, very shy. Naturally tall, I had a perception of myself as overweight as well, and to top it off, I was smart. Tall, fat, smart girls don't date much. I was self-conscious and awkward and had very low self-esteem. Oh, I had some friends, and we did many enjoyable things together, but I always felt out of place.

When I went to college, I picked a school where no one else from my hometown was going. I hoped that I would be able to make a fresh start and leave the "old" me behind. But she followed me—I was still oh so shy. I wanted to break out of my shell and be one of the popular people, but I just couldn't do it.

I was so shy I would cut class if I thought I was going to be late, because I couldn't stand the thought of people looking at me when I walked in. If a stranger talked to me, I blushed. I had a very hard time making eye contact. The only time I was comfortable was when I was being someone else.

In high school, I had discovered debate and declamation and plays. Excelling at these activities allowed me to receive approbation for what I was doing, even though I didn't feel approval for myself as a person. So I got involved in similar activities in college. All I wanted, though, was to be one of the gang, to date, to be thought of as petite and bouncy and cute—things I considered way beyond the realm of possibility.

Once, when I was at a dance occupying my normal wallflower position at the side of the room, I noticed another girl in a similar position. The thought occurred to me: *Why don't I go talk to her? The worst thing that can happen is that she might refuse to talk to me.* I did just that: I went over and introduced myself, we became friends, and that incident started my road toward victory over shyness.

I realized that many people are really shy underneath their calm exterior and that they welcome someone else breaking the ice and talking to them. I realized that if they spurned my attempt at conversation, they had lost the opportunity to make a new acquaintance. From that realization came my practice of talking to and with almost anybody. I have made the best friends and had some of my most wonderful experiences since "talking to strangers" has become my habit.

I began to observe the people around me whom I viewed as having the ability to make friends. One of the best was my dad. He never knew a stranger; they were just friends he hadn't yet met. He didn't view people as superiors or inferiors; they were just "folks." The motto at his place of business was "Howard Wants to See You!" and his customers always felt exactly that way.

After learning to overcome my shyness, acquiring friends and resources became a way of life for me. Knowing who to call for information or to find out how to do something was as important as knowing it myself or having the actual information at my fingertips.

I am now a professional speaker. The "escapes" I used in high school and college became my profession. I am told by many people that they have seen few others who have my ability to speak to an audience of any size and make each member feel as if she is being spoken to personally and individually. I am also told that my audiences feel as if they are a part of my life and that they can become "new best friends" with me if they so desire.

Knowing that I am a person of value and worth has made all the difference in my professional and private life. Being "brave" enough to talk with people has brought me some of the most rewarding experiences of my life. A few years ago, when I was ill, I received email notes from many people I had met on various occasions. They told me that my smile at them or the brief conversations we had engaged in or the introductions I had made for them had benefited them greatly and had made lasting impressions on them.

I am still shy, although most of the people I know would never believe it. However, I operate out of my comfort zone on a daily basis because the benefits far outweigh the risks. Not only do I make new friends and establish new relationships, those people I meet also find others who become friends. By being an example, I have given others the courage to reach out and meet new people and make new friends.

My passion in speaking and writing has become to connect others through positive strategies in communication and networking. I now teach people how to build relationships with others and to network for positive connections.

Deb Haggerty (Florida) is a nationally known speaker whose mission is connecting organizations and individuals through positive strategies in communication, relationship building, and networking. Her books include *The Communication Coach, Half Full,* and *Silver and Gold.* www.DebHaggerty.com

"Pursuing Authentic Dreams"

BY BRENDA POINSETT

My mother embroidered pillowcases frequently when I was a child. The process fascinated me. She would get her iron really hot, unfold the carbon-lined pattern of what she wanted to embroider, lay it on the pillowcase, and press that hot iron on it. Instantly the picture appeared, and then she began working with her threads of greens, blues, reds, and yellows to create a beautiful picture.

As we build our dreams for the future, we need to transfer our vision from our head to somewhere we can see it, embroider it, and bring it to life. I recommend starting with getting your vision on paper. Take what you have in your head and write it down. If you have trouble getting started, here are some ways to begin.

- In my fifties and sixties, I want to be ... or I want to do ...
- By the time I'm seventy-five, I will have wanted to ...
- In my mind, I see myself as a woman who is ... and who will ...
- Over the next twenty years, I want to commit myself to ...

As you study your vision on paper, you may want to refine it to clarify your dream and strengthen your resolve. It also is a good time to ask yourself some tough questions about your vision and then scrutinize it before you go any further by asking:

- Does my vision line up with God's will as revealed in the Bible?
- Can I ask God's blessing on my vision?
- Is this vision one that I could earnestly and prayerfully seek God's help with?
- Does this vision allow me to be myself?

If your vision is God-given it will allow you to be true to yourself. The next years will not be fulfilling if you have to pretend to be someone you are not. Making changes at mid-life does not mean turning into someone you are not. You want to release the real you so your life will be happier and more fulfilling.

This stage of life is time for your uniqueness to flourish—to let your creativity, your convictions, your values, your ideas, and your insights bloom. Being authentic doesn't mean we are perfect, it means not pretending to be perfect. It means admitting we have weaknesses without sacrificing our self-worth. True authenticity also involves a greater awareness of others and a stronger desire for genuine relationships. It means being ready to pursue our own goals even if others ignore or oppose what is important to us.

When I asked our discussion group members to write their goals for the next ten years, one of the participants balked. Overwhelmed by family and financial problems, she shrugged her shoulders and said, "What's the use?"

I understood. I had felt the same way for years. I avoided articles and workshops on goals because I didn't see myself as having choices. My life was wrapped up in being adaptable to the needs of others and keeping bills paid. But now, I was determined to be one of God's spokeswomen, but that was a broad concept. If I wanted to be a deliverer of God's messages and an encourager, how was I going to do that? How would I measure whether I had succeeded?

My vision was short on specifics, but that sense of time running out forced me to make decisions, and I turned my dreams into goals. While writing your vision and/or goals strengthens resolve, so does verbalizing. I told my oldest son and my husband what my goals were. I knew that I would be more earnest about working on them if I did. While I doubt that they would have held me accountable (as in, I thought you were going to …), I felt accountable. Telling them my goals was a miniature commencement ceremony. I was beginning a new life.

But even with 100 percent effort and commitment, we cannot guarantee that our dreams will come true. We don't control all the variables. But the pursuit alone brings energy and vitality into our living. The pursuit is just as important as the result.

To be a spokeswoman for God, and to learn to do it well, I joined the National Speakers Association. When I attended my first NSA meeting, a seasoned speaker took me aside, asked my age, and said, "You need to know that speaking is a very competitive business—very competitive." He could have saved his breath. I had done enough speaking already to know that. Writing is also very competitive. The likelihood that I would fail was great. Since then, I've made blunders and embarrassed myself, but I'm growing, and it is exhilarating. By the standards of others, I still may not be a success, but I can't remember a time in my life when I've felt more fully alive.

From time to time, I go back and look at my written goals. Like a child putting a notch on the doorframe to see how she is growing, I take note of how I've grown. I have almost succeeded in accomplishing my first set of goals, and I have learned so much. I've learned about myself, and I'm seeing my strengths and weaknesses more clearly. I've learned much about speaking and writing. God is opening my eyes in so many ways, and I'm asking Him now what He wants me to aim for next. I anticipate this unfolding process to repeat itself over and over. Always a vision out in front, always growing.

You may be hesitant to follow your dreams because you don't have the necessary skills and knowledge, but returning to school can bring an aliveness to your life. Maybe this is why so many middle-aged adults want to learn; maybe they are hooked on the feeling of aliveness that comes with it. Even when you are striving, stumbling, and struggling, it's exhilarating if you sense you are growing.

You may be frightened to do some of things you have to do in order to see your dream become a reality, but that will prompt you to reach out for God's help. Your faith will be exercised; you will grow spiritually.

Let me repeat: the final result is *not* what is important. What's important are these considerations: Do you have a dream? Are you committed? Can you be true to yourself? Will you feel fully alive striving to reach your potential? Will you grow in the process?

Go for it!

Brenda Poinsett (Missouri) is a teacher, writer, speaker, and organizer whose many books include *Reaching Heaven, Not My Will But Thine, Why Do I Feel This Way?,* and *What Will I Do With the Rest of My Life?* www.yhti.net/~poinsett/brenda.html

"Going Through Changes"

BY SHARON HOFFMAN

Today I suddenly felt old.

A tidal wave of self-pity washed over me. Immediately afterward, a bigger wave of discontent slammed into me. Blows of hurt and plain old rejection soon followed. My nest was not only empty, it was quiet—way too empty and quiet.

Walking past the mirror that day, I spotted a streak of gray, smack in the middle of my bangs. My hair color seemed to have changed overnight. Thank goodness nobody was looking over my shoulder as I paused in the entryway at yet another mirror.

These issues may seem like silly things to cause such a huge blow to my sense of wellbeing. But, the questions in my heart have caused me to do some valuable soul-searching over the past weeks. (Chocolate helped some too!) I have been reminded anew how important it is to base my sense of security and esteem on God and His faithfulness, not on my circumstances or my hormone levels.

I have come to some conclusions—what I call my "five secrets"—that I would like to share with you. I have accepted and am resolved that:

1. My eyesight is not as sharp as it used to be, but I have never seen God's love more clearly. I can trust Him. He has patiently spent many years proving that fact to me. He loves me unconditionally (see Rom. 8:38–39). A vital personal relationship with Him has given me a stronger sense of self-worth at age fifty than I ever had at twenty-one. Then, I thought I could do anything. Now, I know that without Him, I can do nothing (see John 15:5). That's God-confidence, not self-esteem. My eyesight is more sensitive to people; I am much more keenly aware of others' hurts and pain. When a woman knows, as I do, that she is never going to be perfect, she more readily accepts others and is quicker to jump to their rescue when they are hurt or misunderstood.

2. My house is not as bustling with activity as it used to be, but that can be a good thing. I have the time now to pursue new goals and try new things that I never had time for while raising a family. God is opening doors that I dreamed of—providing me many opportunities that have been kept on the back burner for a long time. He is making it clear to me that there is a season for all things (see Eccl. 3:1–12).

3. Aging and physical changes occurring at this time in my life are not necessarily negative and unpleasant; they are just normal. I am finding that prayer, walking, and video exercise classes are a great source of encouragement to me spiritually, as well as physically. Never have I lived on such a beautiful walking path around a lake, and I am taking advantage of it in our lovely southern climate. My health and consistent physical activity as I celebrate my fiftieth birthday are actually superior to those I enjoyed when I turned twenty-five. And my husband says I look the best I have in all our thirty years of marriage. That makes me feel so good. (What is awesome is that I actually think he really believes it!)

4. I know I won't accomplish or acquire everything I thought in my youth that I would. Truth is, there probably isn't enough time left to do all those things. And that has become okay with me. I have learned that things do not define who a person is, nor do they imply a high personal worth. I no longer have to accumulate a lot of clothes, houses, jewelry, or money to be happy. My sense of contentment is not based on my debits/credits list. Embracing the truth that my life is a "vapor" (James 4:14 NKJV, indicating the brevity of life) encourages me to become goal-oriented and to fulfill my God-given purpose on this earth.

5. Outward beauty does not last forever. Glitz and glam are only promises on magazine covers. (Although I never thought I would get those "schoolteacher arms" that flap in the breeze!) Though this outward body is perishing (see 2 Cor. 4:16), at fifty years of age, I am emerging as a different, more insightful woman and am continuing to bloom. I am even enjoying the process. Perhaps it has taken me thirty-one-plus years to grasp the concepts of a Proverbs 31 woman: "Favour is deceitful, and beauty is vain: but a woman that feareth the LORD, she shall be praised" (v. 30 KJV). Looking good on the inside is true beauty because it shows and glows on the outside.

No, a quiet house is not always a bad thing. While I delight in being a mother, I am embarking on a new role—that of grandmother. The joy of training and coaching another generation excites me. An empty nest is a settled nest. Not having to carpool boisterous children and keep up with teens' hectic schedules affords me the opportunity to foster a quiet time with the Lord alone day by day.

My faith has grown from a childish expectation of continual excitement and success to the mature walk of a woman whose journey has been through some of life's deepest valleys, and I have found that I was never alone. God was always right there beside me. I have the luxury of quietness to appreciate the truth that being alone does not have to mean being lonely. I am now afforded the independence that women with biological time clocks can only dream of.

It is not going to be so hard being 50.

Just a few weeks ago, I didn't know these secrets.

Now I do. I have found that turning 50 means that everything in life will change. The greatest changes of all are the gifts I have longed for all my life—within me!

Sharon Hoffman (Tennessee) is the author of five books including *The GIFTed Woman, Come Home to Comfort,* and *Untie the Ribbons.* With an active international speaking ministry, Sharon is president of GIFTed Living—*"helping you to be the very best you can be!"* www.SharonHoffman.com

TRUTH TWO:

God Is in Control

"Out of Control"

BY LUCINDA SECREST MCDOWELL

Hi, my name is Cindy, and I'm a control freak."

"But I am in recovery ... whether I like it or not."

For much of my life I thought that all I had to do was Plan Ahead or Follow the Rules or Check Everything Off the List, and everything would turn out the way it was supposed to. But then life began getting complicated, and all of a sudden everything was spinning "out of control" (meaning of course "out of *my* control").

The truth is that I never was in control; I only tried to be. Someone once said, "Life is what happens while we're busy making other plans." That is true. As I reflect on my first fifty years, I am astonished by the myriad of experiences, relationships and achievements I have enjoyed—none of which I would ever have predicted or pursued.

With increased years, and hopefully some increased wisdom, I now understand that my need to feel in control has roots in insecurity and even pride. God's Word states this truth well in Proverbs 19:21 (CEV): "We may make a lot of plans, but the LORD will do what he has decided."

Recently, while recovering from an accident, I was lying in bed listening to my family at the other end of the room deciding *for me*

49

about everything from how much medicine I should take to what I should eat for supper. It almost drove me crazy.

"Hey," I called feebly from my bed. "I only broke my *leg*, not my *head*. Why don't you ask *me* what I want for supper?"

How we long to cling to the illusion that somehow we still have a say in what happens in our lives. And yet, perhaps one of the greatest lessons I learned during my recent convalescence was that of relinquishment. Being advised that I could not walk or drive for eight weeks definitely changed my plans not only professionally (for the next seven speaking engagements) but also personally (for orchestrating the Thanksgiving and Christmas seasons for my family of six).

I was out of control, and there was nothing I could do about it.

Of course, this has been a lifelong struggle for me. Because my father recorded interviews and performances with his children through the years, we have audio documentation of my arguing with him at age two, "*Me* hold the microphone, Daddy!" Thus began my dubious lifetime endeavor of seeking to take control of any and every situation.

But the unexpected challenges of life force us finally—reluctantly—to recognize that we have no control over our world, our circumstances, and even our loved ones (*especially* our loved ones). And it is at this crucial juncture that each of us must make a choice of whether to spend all our energy scrambling for some semblance of power or to relinquish control to the Creator and Sustainer of the universe.

It was no mistake that I discovered these positive and proactive words by Leonard Sweet in my reading pile during those winter months of enforced isolation:

I am part of the Church of the Out-of-Control. I once was a control junkie, but now am an out-of-control disciple. I've given up my control to God. I trust and obey the Spirit. I've jumped off the fence; I've stepped over the line; I've pulled out all the stops; I'm holding nothing back. There's no turning back, looking around, slowing down, backing away, letting up, or shutting up. It's a life against the odds, outside the box, over the wall, the game of life being played without goal lines other than Thy Will Be Done.

It has taken me almost fifty years to realize that letting go of control will reap benefits in the long run. God, in His infinite wisdom, knew that those eight weeks spent *not* walking and *not* producing were just what was needed for that season of my life. While at the time it made no sense at all, more than a few friends were happy to point out this truth to me.

Perhaps one of the best measures of maturity is the ability to know that God (the One who spun the stars into space) is worthy and willing to take charge of our lives. We can safely leave the future of our world and our loved ones in His capable hands.

Truly God is in control. Whew!

Lucinda Secret McDowell, M.T.S. (Connecticut) presents "Encouraging Words that Transform" through her international conference speaking and writing. A graduate of Gordon-Conwell Seminary, she is the author of five books including *Quilts from Heaven, Women's Spiritual Passages,* and *Amazed by Grace.* www.EncouragingWords.net

"God Is Here"

BY CAROL KENT

The phone rang in the middle of the night and jolted me awake. My husband, Gene, answered, and I soon realized he was receiving devastating news: Our son had been picked up by the police and accused of a serious crime. I couldn't breathe; nausea swept over me. As I tried to stand next to the bed, my knees buckled. *Surely it's a mistake*, I thought desperately. But as the hours unfolded, the circumstances surrounding our son's arrest were validated.

My life's changed dramatically during this extended ordeal. I've watched my dreams for my only child shatter. I've agonized over what I could have done differently as a mother to ensure such a thing would not have happened. Sometimes I feel as though I'm living through an endless Good Friday.

When Jesus died on the cross that Good Friday two thousand years ago, hope (for a moment) was ripped away. Everyone believed He would be the One to redeem Israel from Roman oppression. Then His body was laid in a tomb.

But Easter Sunday arrived. When Mary Magdalene and Mary, Martha's sister, visited Jesus' grave early that morning, they discovered that God's angel had rolled back the stone to reveal a now-empty tomb. The angel told them, "I know you're looking for Jesus, the

One they nailed to the cross. He is not here. He was raised, just as he said. ... Now, get on your way quickly and tell his disciples, 'He is risen from the dead'" (Matt. 28:6–7 MSG). Because of Christ's resurrection, we now have hope that our faith is true, that God can be trusted, and that we, too, will be resurrected (see 1 Cor. 15:13–19).

If I thought for a moment there was no eternity, no heaven, no end to sorrow, no eventual resolution to my personal crisis, I'd want to "check out" right now. But the good news of the Resurrection is the promise that we who believe in Jesus as our Savior will enjoy eternal life in a place free from sorrow, suffering, or tears (see Matt. 25:46; Rev. 21:4).

Incredibly, in the middle of my Good Friday experience, other reasons for hope have emerged. Throughout my family's ordeal, I've learned some lessons that have shown me the same power that brought Jesus Christ back to life is available to us.

Authentic Joy—I didn't expect this first discovery. In the nights immediately following my son's arrest, depression overtook me like a relentless dark cloud. I wanted to retreat into my grief and sleep away the pain. Yet every day when I awakened, the sun came up—and with it, a surprising sense of renewed hope. How dark Good Friday must have seemed to those who loved Jesus! Yet I'm convinced that when the sun rose that Easter morning to reveal the empty tomb, hope replaced darkness and sadness. For no matter how dark the night, Christ's resurrection reminds us that joy comes in the morning (Ps. 30:5).

Jesus promises us, "You will grieve, but your grief will turn to joy" (John 16:20). The friends and family members who've flooded my life with joy in countless ways flesh out this promise for me. For example, days after Gene and I found out about our son, the doorbell rang. There stood a local florist delivering twelve long-stemmed yellow roses. I opened the accompanying note: "You once told us yellow flowers brighten any room. We thought you might need a touch of yellow in your life right now." The note was signed with love from two of my sisters. They had transformed words meant as decorating advice into a gift of joy in my time of crisis! From that point on, my family and friends used yellow—yellow cards, yellow candles, yellow gift-wrapped surprises—to remind me of the Resurrection joy that's available to me in the middle of my journey.

A Faithful Companion—Christ's resurrection ensures that when we enter into a relationship with God as our Father, we have a relationship with Someone who'll never leave us. God is here. Recently I spent several hours with a family of three children who are being raised by their mother. The eldest daughter, Anne, burst into tears as she blurted out, "I'm so angry at my father for leaving us, but I'm even angrier at myself for needing him!" I was able to say confidently as I hugged her, "I know you're hurting because you want to experience your father's love. But you have a relationship with Jesus, who won't ever walk out on you. Remember, Anne, God promises in Hebrews 13:5 that He will never leave you or forsake you."

Power to Overcome—I'd always tried to do my best for God, but when my son was incarcerated, I was humiliated, embarrassed, and ashamed. I felt as though I were a failure as a mother! It was all about me—*my* hurt, *my* pain, *my* devastation, *my* reputation. Only when I looked at my circumstances through the lens of Jesus' death and resurrection did I experience the hope Jesus offers because He arose from the dead.

Freedom from Fear—Stacey came into my life unexpectedly. I spoke at a church in Honolulu not long after September 11, and following my presentation, she asked if we could talk. She explained that she was a flight attendant for United Airlines; Boston's Logan

Airport was her base of operations. "I usually worked one of the flights that hit the World Trade Center, but September 11 was my day off," she said. "I've been so afraid, I took a leave of absence from my job and returned to my home here. I've come to this church to find out how to deal with my fear." I explained to Stacey that because Jesus died for our sins and rose again, God provided a way for us to find forgiveness, hope, and a future free from fear. That day Stacey invited Jesus to come into her life. Her face beamed as she looked up following that prayer.

So there you have it! The good news of the Resurrection means forgiveness of sin, hope for the future, staying power for the tough times, a Father who loves us, eternal life, authentic joy, and freedom from fear. When we get to know the risen Christ personally, we find hope and joy in the midst of our personal Good Fridays. While this good news will change our lives forever, it doesn't stop there. We just naturally have to tell somebody about it. That's why the good news of the Resurrection goes on and on and on.

Carol Kent (Michigan) is an international public speaker and author who is best known for being dynamic, humorous, encouraging, and biblical. Her books include *When I Lay My Isaac Down, Becoming a Woman of Influence, Tame Your Fears,* and *Speak Up With Confidence.* www.CarolKent.org

"At the Window Again"

BY SUSAN ALEXANDER YATES

Once again I was at my front window. This time I watched as Susy and Libby threw their arms around each other and burst into tears.

Twenty of us had just spent a wonderful Easter weekend together. Our kids had brought friends home from college for the holiday. Most of them were freshmen, experiencing their first time away from home. We'd had a great slumber party at our farm, a giant biblical trivia scavenger hunt between "Team Michigan" and "Team Virginia." (Team Virginia won when they found the answer in the Bible to, "Who was the man who ran away naked?") We had sung along with guitars, shared lessons from the year at school, and danced on the old porch. We had attended a wonderful worship service at church on Sunday and had a formal Easter dinner in our front yard!

But now it was time to go, and leaving was so hard. The twins had been apart for the first time this year, and this reunion had been so sweet. But it was over, good-byes had to be said, and the tears flowed freely.

As I watched the girls, my eyes also filled with tears. Tears of joy and tears of sadness. Joy for kids who love each other, joy for their friends who love Christ, joy for this season of teenagers. But there were also tears of sadness. My "babies" were leaving. My nest was emptying out, albeit temporarily. I knew they would be back with more friends and more dirty laundry. But it was the beginning of a new season.

A new season. A season of letting go even more. A season of realizing again and again that I can't "fix things" for them. A season of breakups and start-ups. A season with four kids "in love" at the same time. A season of deepening friendships with adult children. A season of more time for Johnny and me to be together. A season of learning to trust God in new ways.

With this season comes a deep sense of thanksgiving. I am thankful that God is bigger than the mistakes I've made in parenting. Thankful that He knows that I am but dust. Thankful that His strength is perfected in my weakness. Thankful that there is nothing He can't redeem. Thankful that nothing is impossible for Him. Thankful that He loves my kids even more than I do, and that He has a plan for each one of them. Thankful that He also has a plan for me in this new season, as my parenting responsibilities decrease.

Now, I wait at the window for my grandchildren—longing to watch their little feet pound up the walk, waiting to hear them shout, "Ghee and Poppy, here we are!"

What incredible joy.

Susan Alexander Yates (Virginia) is a regular contributor to *Today's Christian Woman* magazine and the author of nine books including *Building a Home Full of Grace* and *And Then I Had Kids*. As the mother of five, she speaks nationally and internationally on marriage and the family. www.YatesBooks.com

"I Don't Want to Learn That!"

BY MARY WILKEN

My six-year-old grandson Kyle spouted his party line for the umpteenth time that day, "It's not fair." So, I launched a grand maternal lecture with, "Kyle, life is not fair; life is hard. If you could learn that at your age, you would be so much happier. You could have a wonderful life." He scowled in contemplation and erupted decisively with a shaking of his head, "Grama … I don't want to learn *that!*"

This was a child of kindred spirit. My husband and I use his profound retort to each other often now. After hearing a challenging sermon or reading Oswald Chambers' devotional, we whisper, "I don't want to learn *that!*" But it doesn't change the fact that life *is* hard at times.

A few years ago we moved from Asheville in the Blue Ridge Mountains to Colorado Springs in the Rockies. By the time we had settled into our new home I couldn't move my left arm. Most motion sent excruciating pain up the length of it. I made an appointment at the doctor's office, and after the initial exam he was baffled. Without any known trauma that could have caused a frozen shoulder at my age, the possibility of cancer was a real concern. He scheduled an MRI and sent me the next day to a physical therapist to start the hard work of regaining the use of my arm. The two weeks I spent waiting for the test results put me in an unreal world of hypersensitivity where I vacillated between overcoming faith and overwhelming fear. There were times when I sensed God's presence literally. I felt very close to Him and experienced His grace and peace in a way I hadn't known in a long time. But occasionally I would be hit with a suffocating fear that brought speculation, anger, and hysterical crying. I felt very alone in a big and bad world.

It turned out that I didn't have a tumor, and after many weeks of tests and therapy I regained the use of my arm. The doctors concluded that perhaps a virus had attacked my nerve plexus, causing the intense pain that was exacerbated by lifting my infant grandson Kristian and moving heavy boxes. To protect myself, I had stopped using my arm, and my shoulder froze from disuse.

I learned so much from my physical therapist. Our bodies are amazing machines. He told me of people who have had severe emotional traumas, like prolonged psychological abuse, which eventually caused physical symptoms. He was unable to help them unless they were willing to deal with the root problems in their lives. One woman eventually died as her body slowly shut down.

Moving away from our hometown of ten years to a new environment helped me gain some objectivity on my spiritual wellness too. I had experienced a lot of emotional challenges during our years in Asheville, and I could see now how I had changed. Somewhere along the way I had gradually lost my joy. My praise and worship had been replaced with persistent cynicism and nagging doubt. I had always had a proclivity to analyze and question things, and some of my experiences in North Carolina seemed only to reinforce my foreboding. Seeing power struggles and rivalry, moral failure and divisions, mediocrity and self-serving attitudes in the church brutalized my trust. Through these many disappointments I came close to giving up on Christianity. At the same time I faced the death of my estranged father and some other challenging personal relationships. I was slowly becoming numb spiritually. I still clung to Christ, but I felt like my faith was adrift—somehow detached from real life and in danger of freezing from disuse.

While our move gave me insight into my condition, and I loved living in Colorado as there were many good things happening in international student ministry there, we went from church to church to try to find a home. By now I could hardly listen to a message without finding some fault with it, and it was the same with praise and worship. I knew I needed to step back and take a long look at my heart. But like my frozen shoulder, my heart seemed paralyzed as a result of my protecting it from pain. On top of all that, difficult things were still happening in our lives, and many of my prayers seemed to go unanswered.

At different times during these months I was challenged with this Scripture when I read it or heard it in a sermon or on the radio: "No longer live as the Gentiles do, in the futility of their thinking. ... darkened in their understanding and separated from the life of God" (Eph. 4:17–18). The J. B. Phillips version says: "Do not live any longer the futile lives of gentiles. For they live in a world of shadows, and are cut off from the life of God." As I started to consider why I was often in the shadow of despair, why I seemed cut off from the life of God, I began to see that so much of my struggle was with my thinking. Looking back, I could see that my anxieties sprang from speculating and wondering about things—letting my imagination create the worst scenario possible and then giving into fear or just trying to figure things out and asking why. In contrast, I knew that God's Word said not to be conformed to the world's ways but to be transformed by renewing our minds (see Rom. 12:2). It seemed to me that living with very little peace and joy was indeed a futile lifestyle for a Christian.

And then we moved again to Phoenix, and after only twelve days, we left for five weeks in the Netherlands where we worked at the Billy Graham conference, *Amsterdam 2000*. My husband and I were responsible for overseeing the feeding of the thousands of participants who stayed at Jaarbeurs, a temporary "city" of bunk beds built for the occasion. It was a daunting task—humanly impossible really—to get seven thousand evangelists awake, served their boxed breakfasts, and on the train to Amsterdam in groups of fourteen hundred. The private trains used to transport them ran in between the public trains, so timing was everything. Some mornings I would stand in the hall as I watched them coming and say to myself, "It's not going to work." But it would work, and God's grace became a visual reality and proved effectively powerful for this situation and for me personally. Time and again when we faced logistical impossibilities, a solution would surface through prayer and dependence on God. This out of the ordinary experience rekindled my faith and hope.

A few months after I had returned to Phoenix, I read a small book that had a great impact on my thinking and removed some shadows about afflictions and suffering as a Christian. *These Strange Ashes* by Elisabeth Elliot tells the story of her first year as a linguistic missionary to the Colorado Indians in Ecuador. She likens this first year and its inexplicable personal losses to her "kindergarten" training as a missionary. These losses included the murder of Macario, the key person to her translation work, because he was the only one known to speak both the Colorado and Spanish languages, and then a stolen suitcase containing the only copy of the Colorado language materials—her work for the salvation of the Indians gone forever.

Reflecting on these incidents she wrote:

Faith's most severe tests come not when we see nothing, but when we see a stunning array of evidence that seems to prove our faith vain. ... To be a follower of the Crucified means, sooner or later, a personal encounter with the cross. And the cross always entails loss.

These poignant lessons assured me I was not alone in my afflictions and my struggle to keep the faith. Trusting God when everything we see and think opposes everything we feel and believe is the challenge for all Christians. But acceptance and a willingness to bow in trust to a God who is sovereign, especially in things we cannot possibly explain in human terms, is the way to freedom. This solution is not the way of survival in this world we humans tenaciously rely on. And like my grandson Kyle, "I really don't want to learn *that!*" but I have come to see that it is the path to keeping my faith alive and giving up my futile ways. At the end of the day, it is the way to abating the shadows and restoring my peace.

That's why my continual prayer to God is: "Restore to me the joy of your salvation and grant me a willing spirit, to sustain me" (Ps. 51:12).

Mary Wilken (Arizona) is a freelance writer and contributing author to *Women's Spiritual Passages*. She works with International Students Incorporated (ISI), welcoming internationals to Phoenix. Married thirty years to Terry, Mary is delighted to have three sons and two grandsons.

"Look Out Below!"

BY PEG CARMACK SHORT

Humble yourselves, therefore,
under God's mighty hand,
that he may lift you up in due time.

1 Peter 5:6

The older I get, the more I realize that just when I think I have everything under control and am holding the world by its proverbial tail—look out below! Something is about to drop on my head. Really, it's true. For example, the higher I climbed the corporate ladder, the more catastrophes befell my husband on his job. At the pinnacle of my career, just when I thought we would be moving to easy street, my husband's employer suddenly declared bankruptcy.

Still hoping to keep us moving upward, I took a job with a new start-up magazine making a salary equal to what the two of us had made together. My job would take up the slack until my husband found new employment, and then we would be back on our way doing better than before. But while I was dreaming of a bigger house that more money would bring us, along came the bust of the dot-com companies followed quickly by 9/11, and suddenly investors were afraid to take chances on new ventures. In a heartbeat, both the new magazine and the company for which I worked vanished along with dreams of our life on easy street. Left with a big mortgage and a lifestyle built on two paychecks, we were moving all right, but in the wrong direction. Unfortunately, life is full of such misadventures.

No one knows that fact better than my friend Barb. She is one of those people to whom missteps just seem to come naturally. No matter how hard she tries to stay in control, things somehow get out of hand—often literally. For instance, a group of us went shopping and stopped at McDonalds to grab a quick lunch. Barb was eating her burger while telling us a funny story, which had us all giggling uncontrollably. Unable to talk without using her hands, she gestured in such a way that the burger popped out of the bun, flew over her shoulder, and landed in the lap of the man behind her ... who just happened to be a police officer in his finest dress blues. Only now they also contained blotches of red catsup, yellow mustard, and a nice slab of green pickle. Barb did her best to apologize while dabbing frantically at his pants leg, which only seemed to smear and set the gooey mess. At least he had a sense of humor. All he said was: "Lady, I hope you aren't the designated driver."

Think this is an isolated occurrence? How about the first time Barb met the mother of her future husband? It was the day he received his graduate degree from college. For several years he had squeezed night classes and homework into a busy travel schedule and a full-time job. His mother was understandably very proud of her son.

After graduation, Barb and her boyfriend Tim joined his family for lunch at a fashionable restaurant. Wanting to impress everyone, Barb was on her best behavior. Things seemed to be going well until Tim's mother asked to see his diploma. Just as he opened it to show his mother, Barb sliced into a stick of cold butter. Her knife struck the plate with such a jolt that the butter slid one way, and the pat she had been slicing flew the other. The pat landed with a splat right on her beloved's hard-earned diploma, leaving behind a nice greasy streak and a furious mother!

That is how life often seems to me. In the midst of some of our brightest days, a stain comes along and mars the perfection. We are hanging onto life with both hands trying to maintain balance, but still everything seems out of control.

Perhaps because I was the youngest in my family, maintaining control of my corner of the world is pretty important to me. But there have been many times in my life when I have had to acknowledge that no matter how hard I tried to hang on, control was simply beyond me. The truth I have learned is that without God in control, my life is *totally* out of control.

Fortunately for those who walk in faith He has promised, "I will never leave you nor forsake you" (Heb. 13:5 NKJV). So when things are slipping out of my grasp, I rest on His promises that I can give all my problems to Him (see 1 Peter 5:7).

During our most recent deep-valley experience, when my husband and I were without a job or prospects, and money was running low, I kept praying, "God, I need a miracle." And one particularly bad day, I am ashamed to say I was chiding Him pretty good and asking, "Did You hear me, Lord?" A few hours later, I went to the mailbox and discovered eleven identical envelopes all from a government agency. Probably some clerical error, I assumed. Instead I discovered that each envelope contained a check righting a mistake I didn't even know had occurred. All the while I was chastising God, He had already provided my deliverance.

Isn't that just like God? He is a wise Father who cares for me.

But before He can do so, I have to surrender control of my life to Him—a step that starts with an attitude of my heart, and one that also requires action. I must be listening, attentive, and responsive. Otherwise, I miss the direction that He has for me. Yet when I allow Him to take charge of my life, things start to change. It isn't that things stop falling on my head, but along with flying projectiles come His finest blessings, because God does cause everything to work together for good to those who love Him (see Rom. 8:28).

Thanks to God, we have finally moved to easy street. However, it wasn't on the path we were traveling. Following Him, we felt led to sell our house with the big mortgage and move to a quiet little town a few hours away. Here an old Victorian house spoke to us. The house, our new neighbors and friends, and even the town itself feel just right to us. After years spent living in the fast lane, it has been like slipping off our shoes and settling into an easy chair—well, actually, it's a porch swing. The stress and hectic pace of our past life has waned, and a new sense of tranquility has replaced it. Daily I thank God for opening my eyes to a direction I never would have considered had He not nudged me here.

Peg Carmack Short (Illinois) is an editor, writer, and speaker who offers encouragement and inspiration on marriage, family, and home. She is the author of *A Country Sampler of Simple Blessings* and *A Still Life—Creating Quiet Spaces for Your Heart and Home.* www.PegShort.com

"Resting Place"

BY SHARON DIETRICH

The chaplain's voice informed me that my twenty-year-old niece did not survive her transplant surgery. Stunned and shaking, I hung up the phone. My first thoughts and prayers were with Patti and Kevin whose only child was gone. Lauren, an angel in disguise, had lived her entire life suffering, fighting the rare illness that eventually took her life. Her pure trust in Jesus and His purpose for her life permeated her spirit and attitude. Her smile, sense of humor, and joy through all the years were unexplainable.

Singer Michael W. Smith once met Lauren and was so taken in by her genuine spirit and love for Christ that he visited her and sent her gifts. When this faithful friend learned of her death, he called and left a message on Lauren's answering machine. In between his tears, he offered a word to Patti and Kevin. "If this is of any help, she just got there before us." Little did Michael know the help this word of comfort would eventually be for us. We serve a sovereign God.

As Lauren's parents and I began making funeral arrangements, I thought, *How does one find a resting place for a twenty-year-old young woman?* I found myself in a cemetery attempting to do just that. I was angry with God in that graveyard, questioning His plan, devastated by Lauren's death, worried about my sister, and wondering if we would survive the pain. My fifty years of living brought no answers, only questions. Tears flowed freely as the three of us walked around a quaint old cemetery. While we knew that Lauren was no longer in her body but with Jesus, we wanted desperately to find just the right resting place.

The search was painful with no clear sense of direction. I offered up a desperate prayer. "Please God, show us where to put Lauren. I know You have a place, and our grief needs some hope. Show us that You are in charge. Show us that You knew beforehand that we would find ourselves in a graveyard. Show us that this is in Your plan and purpose."

My feet moved toward an old tombstone. I read the name: Maggie Watson. My eyes drifted down toward the inscription. It was the only one I read that day. It read: "She suffered all the days of her life, but did not grow faint of heart. She is not gone, just gone before." Michael's words rushed back: "She just got there before us." I could not breathe, my feet were frozen to the spot. Tears flowed. I felt I was standing on holy ground. I called to Patti and Kevin. Patti arrived first. No words were said. None were needed. Kevin joined us and asked, "Did you notice her age?" I had not. "She was twenty-four when she died."

We had found a resting place for one of God's saints.

The fact of God's sovereignty is part of my life, but the proof of His sovereignty on that day still overwhelms me. Maggie Watson died in the 1800s, but on that day God brought a convergence of words, history, and lives to prove His will, His power, and His love. In the 1800s a young woman dies. Her family writes words on a tombstone summarizing her life of suffering and her faith. For two hundred years no one is buried next to her. A friend speaks words of comfort on a machine, and in one profound moment two hundred years disappear—all is present tense. At the time of Maggie Watson's death, God knew that two hundred years later a woman would cry out to Him for a resting place. He knew that a friend's words would tie it all together. God knew. He just knew.

Something else happened in that moment. You see, I was looking for a resting place for Lauren, but in one profound moment I was the one who found the resting place in the midst of the turmoil of my grief. There was no doubt God was in His heaven attending to the smallest detail. My faith and my heart had found a resting place in the tenderness of a God who has also planned my life to the last detail.

Until that day, I had lived the majority of my existence in the present but tense: uptight, anxious, worried, concerned. Blood pressure on the rise, heart and breathing increasing, tense in the present, present but tense. The worries of the moment, the fears of the future, the pressures of succeeding, all these flooded my mind and killed my soul.

Jesus asked a pointed question to us present-tense people in Matthew 6:25,27: "Therefore I tell you, do not worry about your life. ... Who of you by worrying can add a single hour to his life?" In other words, what is your worrying accomplishing? Look at the birds, Jesus says. They don't wake up worried that the worms won't be in the ground or concerned that the robins will get there first and eat them all. Birds simply know that worms will be found. "Are you not much more valuable than they?" (v. 26).

My present-tense living was just a cover-up for the fact that I did not trust God to take care of my family or me. That day the Lord let me know that two hundred years can disappear, and that all is present tense in His eyes. The smallest details do not escape His gaze. My living in the present, tense and anxious, was proof that I did not know how delightful I was and am to my Father.

On that day in the graveyard, I began my journey of trust. Overcoming lifetime habits is not easy, but in this my fiftieth year, I am living out of a resting place. I have discovered that present-tense living is overcome by one fact that has to move from the head to the heart. I am safe in the arms of God at all times, in all moments, in all situations, in all circumstances, in all crises. After fifty years, I am living my life in the present but not tense.

I still have questions about the ways of God. I still miss Lauren and grieve for Patti and Kevin, but I am at peace learning to be present but not tense. My soul is at rest in the hand of a God who knows exactly what to do and when. He can be trusted.

Sharon Dietrich (New Hampshire) is a gifted communicator with a passion for relating the timeless truths of Scripture to today's realities. A sales manager by profession, Sharon is a popular Bible teacher and conference speaker. She loves being a wife and mom.

"Getting Older, Getting Better"

BY SARAH WETZEL

I am not brave. The older I get, the more fears I see in myself. I am not wise. I thought I was wise about twenty years ago, but not now. And now is when I really need wisdom. I am not strong. I used to be strong—strong-willed especially, and strong in opinion and self-confidence. Now I am not so sure of myself. Even though I thought getting older was about getting braver, stronger, and wiser, the words "fearful," "foolish," and "weak" seem to describe me better now, finishing up the fifth decade of my life. And yet God is still growing me up!

Recently I traveled to a small village called Guayaramerín in the Amazon River lowlands of Bolivia. Since I live in a modern city in the highlands of the Andes Mountains, going to the lowlands was a cultural trip for me. Thick humid fresh air. The land of slow down. A step back in time. Transport was either by foot on the red dirt roads or riding sidesaddle on the back of a motorcycle taxi. Hammocks and heat. All air conditioning was natural, as were all the smells.

I volunteered to go to Guayaramerín to teach a workshop on "Grace in the Christian Life" to the women of the area churches at their annual convention. I had much joy in preparing the classes. I had no doubt that God was sending me there, but shortly after I arrived I found that lots of fears had accompanied me: *Who do I think I am? Will I be able to communicate the truths of the gospel as I hoped? Will these people understand my highland-accented Spanish?*

I did not feel adventurous or strong as I barely stayed on the motorcycle seat safely traveling back and forth to the church. All the other ladies perched daintily on the back, nothing touching the driver, but I had to hang on to him for dear life. I explained to each driver why I was clutching his shoulder so firmly. "I am from Cochabamba. I am not used to riding on the back of a moto. Please forgive me for holding on."

"Not to worry, not to worry," one of them told me kindly. "When you are serving the Lord, you have to do lots of new and adventurous things."

He got that right.

In that environment, I felt very foreign, but God showed up. I had confidence and joy in Him, and I felt strong when I stood to teach the truths of grace and the gospel for the Christian life. I had wisdom when I needed it, and I had courage. I enjoyed teaching the workshop, and when it was over, I foolishly thought I had learned the lessons He had for me there.

I was wrong.

The next day I was bumped off my flight because I forgot to reconfirm it ahead of time—something a seasoned missionary in Bolivia like me should not forget. Where was my wisdom? I went back to the airport at 6:00 AM on Monday, and that flight was cancelled due to major mechanical problems with the plane.

"*Mañana,*" they said. *Yeah, right.* I was anxious to get home to attend our annual mission retreat, but there was nothing I could do but wait. *It's all part of the adventure,* I figured. Monday noon I walked back to the airport: the tin-roofed outdoor waiting room connected to a small warehouse and a green wooden control tower on the edge of the red clay landing strip cut out of the jungle. I went to see the man in charge. He was the one who checked in the passengers. He was the one who handled the baggage. He was the one who told me clearly that it was my fault that I missed the first plane. And he was the one who announced the mechanical difficulties and cancelled the Monday flight. He was the only one around: Pedro.

This time Pedro took pity on me and told me that a small plane was coming up from Cochabamba and that if I wanted to, I could return on it that afternoon. *Great!* I was sure that God had sent that plane to get me home in time for the conference.

But that afternoon just after the small plane landed, a terrific windstorm came up, and soon it was raining like it can rain only in the lowland—sheets and sheets of water. Another waiting lady found out what I was waiting for, and she advised me not to get on that small plane in such a storm. But I thought God had sent that plane for me, so if it went, I had to get on it, whether it seemed safe or not.

The pilots were hovering under the tin roof, watching the storm. Miraculously it stopped, and we puddle jumped across the airstrip lugging my two suitcases and a bulky decorative tree trunk that the ladies had given me. We boarded the little six-seater jet, the two pilots and me. While the men did their pre-flight checks, I praised God for His special provision. I was going home.

But it began to rain again, and we got a radio message from the air control tower. "The airstrip is closed until *mañana*." The two pilots looked at each other and shrugged, and then we deboarded down the wet wing, yanked my stuff out of the belly of the plane, and splashed through the red mud and rain back to the tin porch. They told me to wait a bit, while they figured out what time the next day we would depart.

How many times would I say good-bye to Guayaramerín? I was

confused, because I thought God had sent the plane to get me home, but then He sent the storm to keep the plane from flying. "Not to worry," the taxi driver's words came to me. He is definitely the One in charge here.

A few moments later, the rains stopped again, and I watched the pilots go over to the tower and call up to the men at the top. The air controllers leaned out the window, and some lively discussion ensued. Before I knew what was happening, the pilots returned and picked up my stuff saying, "We got permission. Let's go!"

The plane took off right at sunset. It was a most beautiful sky; orange and golden rays beamed through the great blue-gray storm-clouds to the west with bits of clear sky between great cotton clouds to the east. Then we were flying above it all, and quickly the sky darkened into a night softened by the light of the full moon. It was a dream flight. I had no fear. Four hours later I was home.

Adventure done.

As I said, I am not brave. I am not wise. I am not strong. I am not in control. But God does not leave me as I am. Growing old with God is about growing real; about growing in freedom to be human, accepting my weaknesses and facing my fears. It's about knowing where I can get all the bravery and wisdom and strength that I need right when I need it.

I am getting better as I grow older—better at believing and trusting that God is in control.

Sarah Wetzel (Bolivia) enjoys South America where she and her husband Jake and their four daughters have worked in a camp/youth discipleship ministry since 1984. She is a contributing author to *Women's Spiritual Passages*.

Truth Three:

Relationships Are to Be Celebrated

"Just Show Up"

BY LUCINDA SECREST MCDOWELL

I know you said not to come, but God told me differently," announced my best friend, Maggie, who had driven three hours on Easter weekend to sit with me during my husband's unexpected open-heart surgery.

"But you're a pastor's wife too, with five teenagers at home. You can't afford the time to be here right now," I protested.

And yet, here she was.

The day before, when we discovered that Mike needed five bypasses, I felt scared, but strong. "I can do this," I murmured while phoning kids, parents, and other family members—all thousands of miles away from our New England pastorate.

But Maggie's arrival just outside the operating room was truly a gift I needed, whether or not I realized it. For seven hours on Good Friday, we sat, prayed, and talked until the heart surgeon arrived to tell us all had gone well.

As I collapsed with relief into Maggie's arms, I knew God's faithfulness would continue on the long journey ahead for Mike and me. But, for tonight, I wasn't alone.

Because Maggie showed up.

Do you have a friend like that? Perhaps a better question for all of us is, "Am I a friend like that?"

The longer I live, the more I am convinced that what truly matters are the moments we spend with significant people in our lives. As time moves so quickly, we often look back with regret at the times we neglected family or friends. Our parents begin to age, and we realize with incredulity how much they actually know. Our children become adults and move on, while we eagerly hope to maintain some significant part in their busy lives. And if we still have old friends around, we should consider ourselves quite lucky to have weathered so much change and still be able to laugh and linger over tea.

Author Anna Quindlen tried to emphasize this point in her recent address to the graduating class of Villanova University:

Here is my resume. I am a good mother to three children. I have tried never to let my profession stand in the way of being a good parent. I no longer consider myself the center of the universe. I show up, I listen, I try to laugh. I am a good friend to my husband. I have tried to make marriage vows mean what they say. I show up, I listen, I try to laugh. I am a good friend to my friends, and they to me. Without them, there would be nothing to say to you today, because I would be a cardboard cutout. But I call them on the phone, and I meet them for lunch. I show up, I listen, I try to laugh.

I would be rotten, or at best mediocre at my job, if those other things were not true. You cannot be really first rate at your work if your work is all you are. So here's what I wanted to tell you today: Get a life, a real Life, not a manic pursuit of the next promotion, the bigger paycheck, the larger house. Do you think you'd care so very much about those things if you blew an aneurysm one afternoon, or found a lump in your breast? Get a life in which you are not alone. Find people you love, and who love you, and remember that love is not leisure, it is work.

Just before my fiftieth birthday, I put together a memory scrapbook of "My First 50 Years." Yes, it's quite thick, but it was important to me to document significant people and places in my life thus far. It was truly a celebration of God's faithfulness to me. But there were three dear friends born about the same time I was who never reached this significant milestone. My college roommate, Chris, was killed in a car accident while in her twenties. My prayer partner, Jill, died of a brain tumor in her thirties. And my lifelong best friend since age two, Cax, died violently by her own hand in her forties. I still miss them all.

People are what matters most. So celebrate your relationships today. Write a letter. Make a phone call. Take someone to lunch. Go out of your way to encourage and appreciate family and friends, colleagues and neighbors. Laugh, cry, but most of all, just show up.

Lucinda Secrest McDowell, M.T.S. (Connecticut) presents "Encouraging Words that Transform" through her international conference speaking and writing. A graduate of Gordon-Conwell Seminary, she is the author of five books including *Quilts from Heaven, Women's Spiritual Passages,* and *Amazed by Grace.* www.EncouragingWords.net

"We Need Each Other"

BY RUTH SENTER

Why do we need to stay connected with other women?

It is fantasy to believe we will always be strong. Even the strongest among us will someday face something that will cause us to wilt like a daisy in the sun. Sooner or later something will drain the self-assuredness right out of our veins.

What then? Who will be there for us then?

Oh yes, family will be there. But when pain runs in my blood, it runs in the blood of all my family. Who will be there as a friend, caring deeply for me but separated enough from my pain to look at things realistically? Who will keep a level enough head to point me in the right direction? That's what connectedness is all about—somebody to lean on.

But we must also stay connected for the sake of what we can learn from each other—for the incredible amount of knowledge, wisdom, and information other women can pass on to us.

How fortunate for us when we can learn from each other. We get double value. We get our experiences, plus another's. We get our thoughts, plus someone else's. We get what we have learned through the years *and* what another has learned through the years.

Think how in touch with the past we could be if we stayed in touch with each other. We could be the conveyors of memories for each other and for each other's children. We could say, "Remember when …" and then laugh and cry and tell the stories once again for our offspring to hear.

Sometimes the world is big and wide and scary, even to the most confident of us. There is something secure about someone holding your hand when the crowd is pressing in on you. You are not as likely to be swallowed up or pulled along. Someone will know if you happen to disappear, and they will come looking for you. Connectedness comforts the child in us.

The time has come for women to reconnect. It is time for us to remember each other. To humbly admit how much we need each other. To commit the details of remembering what is going on in another's life. Important dates. Prayer requests. Tough assignments coming up.

To commit to hanging on to each other so that one or the other of us doesn't slip. And if we notice a slide beginning, to lovingly and gently point to the consequences.

To always be there for each other, never running away in fear or hurt. And if fear or hurt is threatening to break off connections, to mentally take note and say to the other, "I need you. Please. What can we do to fix this?"

It is time we stay connected, no matter what, hanging on to one another the way God patiently hangs on to us. "For I am convinced that neither death nor life, neither angels nor demons, neither the present nor the future, nor any powers, neither height nor depth, nor anything else in all creation, will be able to separate us from the love of God that is in Christ Jesus our Lord" (Rom. 8:38–39).

I have never met Mother Teresa. But I have been in the same room as her. Granted, it was a very large room. And from where I was sitting, I could not really look into her eyes. But I felt she was looking into mine. Her voice was thin, her accent thick. But I don't think I've ever had words impact me more.

Her words were not all that impacted me.

It was a grand meal we were treated to that day. But Mother Teresa was nowhere to be seen while we ate. She did not sit at the head table with the other notables. Afterward I learned she had been down in the basement eating rice with the sisters of her order.

In this day when we are more likely to be off caring for ourselves, caring about ourselves, eating at the "head tables," Mother Teresa's example is not to be overlooked.

She never forgot her sisters.

And she was willing to sit in the basement with them and eat rice rather than feast on the riches of the limelight.

May God grant us the courage to do likewise.

Ruth Senter (Illinois) is a national conference speaker and the author of eleven books including the Angel Award winner, *Have We Really Come a Long Way?* She has served in editorial positions for many Christian magazines and as a regular columnist for *The Christian Reader.*

"Learning to Be a Comforter-Friend"

BY GAIL MACDONALD

In Luke 4:18–19 (TLB) Jesus set the direction of His early ministry by reading from Isaiah. "The Spirit of the Lord is upon me; he has appointed me to preach Good News to the poor; he has sent me to heal the brokenhearted and to announce that captives shall be released and the blind shall see, that the downtrodden shall be freed from their oppressors, and that God is ready to give blessings to all who come to him." If I break out the verbs of that reading from all the other words, I hear Jesus saying that He came to comfort, rescue, release, and heal. But should not these tasks belong to those who follow Him as well? Christ's dream seemed to be that succeeding generations would do this task in an even greater and larger scope than He did.

This kind of comforter-friend is never seen more clearly than in Jesus' prediction of Simon Peter's denial on the night of the Crucifixion. He warned Peter that he was going to fail, but did not prevent His disciple from failing. That is important. While He may not have wanted it to happen, *Jesus let Peter fail.*

The words that came next from Jesus were, "Do not let your hearts be troubled" (John 14:1). I believe there is no coincidence in this word placement. For Jesus was looking beyond the failure to the possibilities that would come afterward. He was already looking toward the time of restoration when the lessons learned from the failure would be sorted out and welded into Peter's soul. Jesus, the Comforter-Friend, thought long term—before, during, and after the fall. Most of us do not.

Not all of us are capable of being such a comforter-friend. The fact is that many of us don't know *how* to comfort. Some of us are afraid to try.

One day I asked a friend if, when her house burned to the ground, her friends were there for her. Some, yes, she said. Others, whom she thought were close friends, had avoided saying even one word to her. This "shunning" made things worse because it appeared that they were indifferent to her pain. In truth, they probably felt inadequate, not knowing what to say or do—they didn't have answers.

At such times, when comforting others is hard, we need to realize that a hug, a touch on the arm, a short prayer, or even a brief remark like, "I'm at a loss for words, but I care about you" helps immensely.

Each person's needs, how we express them, and how we wish to be comforted, all differ. I'm the kind who would like a few friends to walk *through* my dark times with me, but it's important to me that they not offer pity. I want them to challenge me to face the pain and encourage me to persevere.

I know others who prefer to keep their pain to themselves. In their anguish, they would like to be left alone. When you know such a person, you can only assure him or her that you're available and will check in from time to time and send notes to encourage instead. Yet, I have never met a person who didn't need the touches and prayers that reassure that there is life beyond these days of numbing limbo.

It's impressive that when Jesus was headed for the awful hours on the cross, He made no move to generate sympathy from the disciples. He *did*, however, want them close by: "Watch with Me," and "Pray with Me."

The true comforter-friend comes alongside and offers herself as a companion in the pain or distress. Not a sermon. Not a cliché. Not an analysis. Not even an I-told-you-so. Just herself.

Gail MacDonald (New Hampshire) is an author, speaker, and counselor to women in leadership as well as a speaker for Focus on the Family's pastors' wives conferences. Her books include *In His Everlasting Arms*, *The Heart of the Master*, and *High Call, High Privilege*.

"Heart Gifts"

BY JENNIE AFMAN DIMKOFF

One spring my husband, Graydon, planted an entire flat of thirty-six little tomato plants in our backyard garden. The summer that followed was exhausting because he was running for a judgeship position, and every weekend found us campaigning until we dropped. August came, and we were overwhelmed with tomatoes.

One hot, humid afternoon the Bivinses stopped by. Jenny Bivins was our daughter, Amber's, very best friend. The five-year-old girls disappeared upstairs to play, and Char Bivins and I sat on the front porch to visit, with our toddlers playing on the floor beside us.

"I wish I knew one more person who could use a tomato," I sighed. "I have given them to everyone I can think of, and they are rotting on the vine!"

"I'll can them," Char replied.

"You have got to be kidding," I responded. Char was well along her third pregnancy, and besides that, it was miserably hot and humid.

"I mean it," she said.

"Char, if you want those tomatoes for your own use, you can have them all. I'll pick them, load your car, and you can borrow my canning jars for a year. I don't have time to use them this year."

Several weeks went by. I pulled in my driveway one day after a speaking engagement, and sitting on the wide, front step was a worn, familiar-looking box. *Looks like she didn't need all those jars after all,* I thought.

The box was heavy and full of wonderful things. There were jars of canned tomatoes, peaches, pears, green beans, pickles, and even a jar of jalapeño peppers! However, what made them extra-special were the pieces of paper of various sizes that were taped on each jar. In Char's handwriting were verses of scripture, lines of poetry, or little notes of encouragement.

I called her up.

"Thank you, Char. You made a practical gift so special! I love you for that."

Just a few weeks later we learned that our friends, the Bivinses, were moving to another city. I tucked five-year-old Amber in bed the first night after hearing the news. Folding her hands tightly together, her earnest prayer began:

"Dear Lord, please be with my friend Jenny when she goes to her new kindergarten and I'm not there. Please help her not to be lonely or afraid. And please, Lord, be with me when I go to my kindergarten and Jenny's not there. I just know I'll cry and cry—in fact … I think … I'll just start … right nowwwwww!"

And together we cried because our friends the Bivenses were leaving.

My friend Char would never know the particular days she ministered to me: Days when I reached for a jar of her canned goods to enhance the "burnt offering" I was placing before my own family. Rushed days. Frustrating days. On ordinary days, when her simple words of encouragement on jars of canned goods lifted my spirits and touched my heart.

Jennie Afman Dimkoff (Michigan) is the president of Storyline Ministries, a trainer for *Speak Up With Confidence* seminars, a national conference speaker, and the author of several books including *Night Whispers: Bedtime Bible Stories for Women.* www.JennieDimkoff.org

"Praying Together"

BY CHERI FULLER

Early in our marriage and our faith journey, Holmes and I experienced difficulties, which brought us to our knees, literally. When we had tried all else, we prayed together, and God answered. But God's direct answer to our prayer, wonderful as it was, was not the most important result of our praying together. Even more precious was that our hearts began to be knit together through the incredible closeness we felt as we prayed to our Father.

Without a counselor to tell us what was wrong, God Himself began to heal our marriage. And with every prayer we prayed together, Jesus became that third strand of a braided cord, binding us tightly together and giving us strength. With this increased spiritual bonding came emotional intimacy. The heart-to-heart connection with my husband that I had desired for so long slowly began to become a reality.

We've traveled down the road a ways in the intervening twenty years as we've talked to the Lord about a myriad of concerns. We've prayed our kids through chicken pox, asthma, broken bones, stitches, and painful ear infections. We've asked God such questions as "Where should we send our children to school?"

and "Should we sell the house?" We've prayed through business storms, school problems, driver's ed, and prom nights. We've also prayed certain girlfriends and boyfriends out the door—and others in!

We have asked for wisdom when we were fresh out of it, especially when navigating our kids through the rough waters of adolescence. As the years passed, our sphere broadened as we prayed for extended family, friends, missionaries, and others. We've prayed for people who needed God's love, help, and healing at church and on mission trips. And countless times we've thanked God for another day of life and for the bounty and blessing of sharing an evening meal or a picnic in the park together as a family.

Sometimes we've talked to the Lord aloud as we drove across the country. Other times we've held hands and prayed silently when there were no words—when both of us lost parents within a two-year span and as our first grandbaby lay in critical condition in the neonatal intensive care unit. We've knelt to utter innumerable prayers of *I'm sorry, God; I've blown it again.* And more than once we've prayed the "Jehoshaphat" prayer: *Lord, we don't know what to do, but our eyes are upon You.*

We've seen firsthand that praying as a couple *works!* There is a special effectiveness and power released when ordinary husbands and wives like us agree in prayer. Maybe that's why Satan likes to keep us all so busy that we often have to expend some extra effort to make it happen.

My husband and I have discovered a special, heart-to-heart connection that is only available through prayer and spiritual interaction. When we're fresh out of love and patience with each other, God has an inexhaustible supply of each, ready and waiting for us to ask. And although we've seen Him work in our lives and our children's lives over and over as we've prayed, we still have not arrived. We are still whispering, *Lord, teach us to pray*. And we're still finding that He loves to show us more!

Cheri Fuller (Oklahoma) speaks internationally through her ministry, Families Pray USA. A contributing editor for *Today's Christian Woman* magazine, she is an award-winning author of many books including *Loving Your Kids While Leaning on God, The Mom You're Meant to Be,* and *The One Year Book of Praying Through the Bible*. www.CheriFuller.com

"I Do Dance, Just Ask Me!"

BY LYNN D. MORRISSEY

As is often my custom when taking a break from writing, I turned up the volume on some spirited praise music and began to dance up a storm. Unknown to me, my daughter Sheridan's five-year-old buddy, Austin, had left her in the family room and was watching my performance, wide-eyed and wide-mouthed. "*What are you doing?*" he ventured, incredulously.

"Why dancing, of course, Austin. Would you and Sheridan like to join me? She often does."

"My mother doesn't dance. And you're too old to dance!" Out of the mouth of babes ...

I have never been any good at dancing, and now at fifty, I'm still not, but at least I've *tried* and will keep on trying—without the help of my friends like Austin, or even the help of my beloved.

Unfortunately, I married a man who routinely parrots Fred Astaire's response once to Ginger Rogers, "I won't dance; don't ask me."

Though I knew that Michael had meant what he said, I decided that not asking did not include begging, cajoling, needling, or pushing. Unfortunately, my prodding backfired, and he began pushing back—literally—on the dance floor.

Witness the many times we went to wedding receptions: After

consuming all the buffet fare, cake, and punch, I could hold, I would drag Mike, kicking and screaming, onto the dance floor. After stilted attempts at slow dancing (though he was very skilled at stepping on my feet), Mike would literally shove me into other couples across a crowded room, proclaiming this admonition loudly enough for everyone to hear: "Lynni, stop pushing!" Embarrassed, I would quickly retreat and follow Michael to our table, gladly taking my seat.

These occurrences escalated until they reached one final, humiliating climax. My boss of many years was leaving the agency and invited Michael and me to a special retirement celebration at, of all places, a disco restaurant. Michael agreed to go without too much protest, which surprised me. However, I also realized that he didn't have much choice.

After dinner, couples began to gather on the dance floor under bright lights and a spinning, mirrored globe. After my repeated urgings, Michael reluctantly followed me center-stage, but before stepping onto the floor, he whispered this ominous warning into my ear: "Lynni, this sounds like one of those songs that starts out slow and ends up fast, and if it does, I just want you to know that I am leaving to sit down." Uncanny. After hearing only a few notes sung by popular disco diva, Donna Summers, Michael had intuitively known the score. But I didn't. I thought he was surely bluffing. The song was slow, and it did get fast, and right on cue as promised, he most certainly did sit down.

The only problem was that I didn't. I stood speechless, motionless, incredulous—*mortified*. How could Michael be so low as to let me solo? I tried quickly to escape, but was bumped from one rump to the next until I didn't know which end was up. (No pun intended.) As I tried to grope my way through the gyrating group,

I suddenly realized that they weren't any more oriented than I. None seemed paired off, and each reveled in his or her independent disco dynamics. These folks were actually having a better time without a partner.

I took my cue and kicked up my heels (and without Michael around to push, I didn't end up kicking anyone else in the process). I had a marvelous time. I suddenly realized that he really *didn't* dance, so no longer would I ask him. I could have fun by myself.

Since the day long ago that I learned that I *do* dance (please ask me!), I have continued to soul-strut around the house to praise music's greatest hits. What an uplifting experience I have as I dance "as unto the Lord." I feel such joy as I worship God in free-spirited frolic.

Sometimes ten-year-old Sheridan joins me. We have a fabulous time dancing, singing, and making a joyful noise (and spectacle of ourselves) to the Lord. When I am tempted to feel somewhat silly, especially at "my age," I am reminded of how King David, worshiping in total self-abandonment, "danced before the LORD with all his might, while he and the entire house of Israel brought up the ark of the LORD with shouts and the sound of trumpets" (2 Sam. 6:14). David said, "I will celebrate before the LORD" (2 Sam. 6:21). I celebrate too, and I know it's all right. It is pleasing in God's sight.

As for Michael, he has discovered that God is no respecter of persons. Since he wouldn't agree to dance in public with his wife, God has made him dance anyway—with his daughter. Every Valentine's Day, he is under strict obligation to accompany Sheridan to the Ritz-Carlton to be her dancing partner at the Cupid's Ball. He *still* doesn't dance (oh, please don't ask him!), but Sheridan doesn't seem to know the difference.

Although I do know the difference—that neither Michael nor I really dance very well—I don't think it *makes* a difference. I fully intend to keep dancing for the next fifty years. After that, I have a feeling I'll be dancing on heaven's streets with the Lord of the dance Himself as my partner, and that will make all the difference.

Lynn D. Morrissey (Missouri) is the author of *Love Letters to God*, devotionals *Seasons of a Woman's Heart* and *Treasures of a Woman's Heart*, and contributing author to numerous best-sellers. She is a CLASS speaker and member of AWSA specializing in prayer journaling. words@brick.net

"Blessed to Be a Blessing"

BY ANNE GRAHAM LOTZ

In the Bible, water often symbolizes blessing. A river of water not only flowed *into and through* Eden, it flowed *from* Eden. In other words, the first home was a blessed place, and blessing flowed from it to the surrounding area.

Our homes have been blessed to be a blessing to others. One way we have sought to receive God's blessing in our home is through putting Him first, acknowledging Him in all we decide and do, loving Him with all our hearts, spending time with Him in His Word and prayer, talking about Him during the day—totally living our lives for Him. Then we seek to impart His blessing to others, not only by getting involved in church and community activities but through hospitality—inviting people in for meals or games or Bible studies and prayer.

When my youngest daughter became engaged this past Christmas, I invited forty friends to come celebrate with us. I asked the guests to bring with them a Bible verse written out on a card that would express their desire or wish for the young couple. Following a time of joyful conversation and dessert, the guests were gathered together and each was asked to share his or her verse out loud.

Some guests gave gifts that illustrated the verse they shared.

One friend shared Ecclesiastes 4:9–12: "Two are better than one, because they have a good return for their work: If one falls down, his friend can help him up. But pity the man who falls and has no one to help him up! Also, if two lie down together, they will keep warm. But how can one keep warm alone? Though one may be overpowered, two can defend themselves. A cord of three strands is not quickly broken."

Her gift to illustrate these truths was a beautiful, three-stranded gold cord from which hung a gold cross. I know as my daughter hangs the gold cord and cross in her new home, she will constantly be reminded of the strength God Himself will infuse into her marriage as she and her husband wind themselves around God and keep the cross central in their relationship. As one by one our friends read and explained their verses, I was consciously aware that the entire room was saturated in God's blessing! When the guests left later in the evening, without exception as they walked out the door, they shared what a blessing they had received. The "river" had flowed through our home, to our children, and out to our guests.

We have used this same simple format on a variety of occasions, asking guests to share a verse that has been meaningful to them, and we have shared our verses with guests. Sunday dinners, birthday parties, anniversaries, or any occasion when we have guests becomes richer and more meaningful as we place God at the center. The gatherings are prayerfully planned as we seek God's blessing on our home as well as on those who enter it that the "river" might flow fully and freely. Again and again we have been "drenched."

Many homes today seem to be preoccupied only with those who live within their walls. Parents either hover over their children, making sure they dress the right way, have just the right friends, and go to just the right parties, smothering them to the point that the children become so wrapped in selfishness that they are not a blessing to anyone. Or children are totally neglected by parents who pursue their own selfish goals. Left to their own devices, very rarely do neglected children, who are not consciously aware of any blessings coming into their lives, become a source of blessing flowing out to others.

The first home in Eden was not only beautiful, it was blessed to be a blessing. May our lives do the same.

Anne Graham Lotz (North Carolina), the daughter of Billy and Ruth Graham, is an international Bible teacher and award-winning author of five books including *Just Give Me Jesus, Heaven: My Father's House, God's Story,* and *My Heart's Cry.* www.AngelMinistries.org

"Resident Alien"

BY MARJORIE WALLEM ROWE

I never met her, but I certainly knew her name well: Bertha Nygaard. I have never visited the place of her birth, but I felt I knew it well: Bergen, Norway. Like a child eager to discover a new treasure, I carefully typed the name into the computer file labeled Passenger Search, pressed "enter," and waited for the past to unfold.

As a fifty-year-old woman, I have used computers for years as if they were glorified typewriters. Word processing was great and email a blessing (and sometimes a curse). As for the Internet, however, I avoided it entirely. The perfectionist in me shied away from the avalanche of information I feared would overwhelm me, while the procrastinator in me simply did not want to deal with it at all.

What finally drove me to dive in and "surf the Net" was a longing to find my grandmother, a woman I had never known. My father's mother immigrated to America from Norway in 1905 and established residency here. She worked in Chicago for a number of years as a single woman while making several trips home to Norway to visit her family. In 1920 at the age of thirty she married my grandfather, and together they established a home for the five children who arrived during the course of the next fourteen years. By 1935 she was dead, victim of a deadly pneumonia that took her life in the Illinois farmhouse where I grew up.

All my life I had known only these bare facts about the life of the woman who was mother to my father—a woman who died at the age of forty-five, leaving behind five young children and a grieving husband. The only images I had of her were grainy black and white photos taken when she was still a teenager. *How tall was she?* I wondered. *What color were her hair and eyes?* Occasionally older relatives would comment that I was the grandchild who most resembled her, but she died when she was younger than I am now. *Who was she really?* I wondered.

What I didn't have to wonder about was her faith. She was a kind woman, my father remembered, one who always made time to nurse a sick neighbor or listen to a stranger in need. While working in Chicago as a governess, Bertha met the man who was to become my grandfather. He had been introduced to Christ through the ministry of Moody Church. Together they established a household of faith, their large Norwegian Bible their prized possession.

The old farmhouse held little else of value. Times were hard in those Depression days, and my grandparents had little money. When I began my search, I had no books, no papers, and no item of jewelry to give me any information about my grandmother. All I had was her name and a desire to know something more about this woman I was said to resemble.

What is it about growing older that makes us hungry to discover family we never knew? When we are young, our attentions are consumed by our friendships or by the immediate family that surrounds us. As we age, though, it is as if we are reawakened by a need to connect with or learn from our past. Family history takes on new meaning. Reunions are attended most eagerly by those who have lived long enough to appreciate the brevity of life.

Just as we can develop an appetite for the past, it is also possible to become homesick for a place we have never been. In my forties I became increasingly aware of a restlessness within me—a desire to go home. *But where was home?* I wondered. I grew up in Illinois, and yes, my parents were still there, but New England had been our adopted home for nearly twenty-five years. What was I looking for? I was surrounded by husband, children, and friends of many years' standing; why did I no longer feel at home?

The answer came suddenly, and from an unexpected source. A friend's child had gone away happily to Christian camp one summer, only to become so miserably ill with homesickness that his parents had to collect him. When I heard this, my mind flashed back to 1963, and to memories of myself as a little girl nicknamed Marji.

That summer I, too, went away to a camp not far from home. Having grown up fairly isolated on the farm, however, it was much too far for me. I cried and pined for my parents and was unable to eat or sleep, so my parents had to be summoned to fetch me. It wasn't easy to admit to surprised adults at church that Sunday that I had simply been too lonely to stay apart from my folks. "I was sick for home," I explained feebly, "and they let me come."

Longing for home at age ten is one thing; at age fifty, quite another. Yet as I remembered in my mind's eye the little girl whose parents' compassion allowed her to return home, I envisioned with sudden clarity another scene. Another homesick child. Another homecoming.

I saw my grandmother, the woman I had never met, waiting for me in heaven. When she saw me, her face first registered joy and then perplexity. "Why, little Marji," I imagined her saying, "I thought you were at Life Camp."

"Oh, Grandma," I replied with elation. "I got sick for home, and the Father let me come."

This scene came to me one day with such sudden clarity that it drove me to my Bible. Sure enough, the answer I was looking for was there. "Dear friends," wrote the apostle Peter, "I urge you, as aliens and strangers in the world. ... Live ... good lives among the pagans ..." (1 Peter 2:11–12). *Aliens,* I mused as I put down my Bible and gazed out the window. *We are aliens here. We are in the world but not of it. No wonder I so often feel homesick!*

It was shortly after that epiphany that my longing to know more of my grandmother drove me to explore the caverns of the Internet for the first time. With a thrill of excitement I discovered a web site devoted to archival records of those immigrants who came to America during the early years of the twentieth century. I entered my grandmother's name and waited. In just seconds a site popped up asking whether I would like to view an image of the original manifest from the ship, the *Bergensfjord,* on which Bertha Nygaard came to America. Bertha Nygaard, the woman who would one day give birth to my father, was line #0005.

I began to read the responses that my grandmother had given to the questions put to her so many years ago: Who paid her passage? Herself. Did she have money in her pocket? Yes. Did she have a place to stay? Yes, in Ottawa, Illinois, with her married sister who had come over years before. And then the physical description: hair, blonde; eyes, blue; height, five feet six inches. My hair, my eyes, my height precisely! And then stamped in bold black ink nearly a century ago, "Resident Alien."

Oh, Grandma, I thought with tears in my eyes, *I never knew you. You died so young. You left a husband and five children. I have a husband and five children. You came to America to find a better life; I came to New England for the same reason. You loved and served the Lord your God. So do I!*

My grandmother died nearly twenty years before I was born, but that day she taught me a lesson without price. I, too, am a "resident alien." This world is not my true home, but for the brief time I am here, I have a responsibility to use my years wisely and well.

Grandma did not live to see her fifties, but her granddaughter has. These additional years are a gift from the One who is our Father. The day will come when Life Camp will be over, and I will be called home. Until then, I will treasure each day as the gift from God that it truly is.

Grandma, I think, would be pleased.

Marjorie Wallem Rowe (Illinois) is a college communications instructor and freelance writer who has contributed to several books. As a pastor's wife and mother of three, Maggie also speaks and performs evangelistic drama at retreats and conferences across the nation. Maggie_rowe@ameritech.net

"Pity Party"

BY JANET HOLM MCHENRY

It was definite. I had decided. And that was that! I was not going to have a Pity Party for my fiftieth birthday. After all, I had been there, done that for my fortieth.

As that decade had loomed, my husband Craig had asked, "Do you want a party for your fortieth?"

"No," I said hastily. "Why would I want to celebrate the fact that I'm joining the middle aged? Forget it—no party!"

But I was wrong. There *was* a party for my fortieth. Ah, there were no balloons, no streamers, no cake, no "Happy Birthday to You." Instead, it was a Pity Party, and I was the only guest. And what good is a Pity Party when you are all by yourself?

So, I had decided that I would instead enter into the sixth decade of my life differently. I would *welcome* any and all suggestions for a birthday party, a dinner out, those oh-so-embarrassing flowers delivered at the high school where I teach—anything.

Bring it on! I prayed.

But in my plans I failed to do one thing. I failed to tell someone I love to have a party for me. I failed even to remind my husband that a certain important date was approaching, since I usually have to post neon signs all over the house as reminders for impending

Hallmark occasions. And as it turned out, I wasn't even going to be home for my birthday; I was headed out of town for a speaking engagement. So even if friends had something cooking, I wouldn't be there for even a taste.

As the date was just a few days ahead, I decided instead to focus on the more spiritual aspects of birthdays, especially ones with zeroes in them. I decided to make the days of my March birthday week a spring Thanksgiving. Every day, every hour if possible, I would find a reason to thank God.

Here are some of my fiftieth spring Thanksgiving prayers I said that weekend:

Thank You, Lord, that I didn't lose those pounds I planned, so I don't have to spend all that money replacing my clothes.

Thank You, Lord, that I forgot the shoes I was going to wear when I go to speak. Now I can wear my teenybopper shoes and make fun of myself.

Thank You, Lord, that I am much younger than most of my audience.

Thank You, Lord, that only half of them are falling asleep.

And so on. I was not about to start any fiftieth Pity Party. Oh, no.

Right after the luncheon, I headed to my mom's house, where I would pick up my daughter Bethany, who was waiting for me to take her and a van load of cousins to the skating rink for her ninth birthday. Yes, Bethany was my late-in-life birthday present, born just a few days before I turned forty-one. Since Bethany was my emotional mirror image, I knew her day was important to her, so I had arranged a special party for her, complete with a Baskin-Robbins cake.

I was after all the Queen of Birthday Parties. I even taught myself cake decorating when my oldest approached her first birthday. I have made cakes shaped like horses, rainbows, Mickey Mouse, bears, The Count, a cowboy—you name it, I have sprayed a thousand frosting stars on it.

And I fashioned the parties to match. The cowboy cake came with blue enamelware dishes, red bandana napkins, a shooting gallery, gold panning, and cowboy and Indian costumes. I believed in making memories.

Bethany's day included many memories for her ninth birthday. Roller-skating with about two thousand other kids also celebrating birthdays on a couple of dozen lined up tables. Older cousins who ignored her. Younger cousins who were too scared to skate. Cardboard pizza. Melting cake. Spilled soda.

It might have turned into a Pity Party, except for presents all wrapped up nice and "Happy–Birthday–to–You," and a big button with Bethany's picture on it. Soon everyone was filled with pizza and cake and soda and skating and video games, but there was one problem. My brothers and sister hadn't showed up to pick up their kids, as they said they would. We waited inside, then we waited outside, then I telephoned around.

Refusing to give in to the Potential Pity Party, I remembered my decision to have a spring Thanksgiving that week:

Thank You, Lord, for the opportunity to do additional bonding with my wonderful nieces and nephews as I drive them all to my mom's house and then baby-sit them until my negligent siblings finally show up!

Grrrrrrr.

But the kids were good on the way to Mom's, and I felt a twinge of guilt … that is, until I actually drove up in front of the house to find both my brothers' and my sister's cars there parked in the driveway.

Grrrrrr. Hadn't they remembered how tired Queen of Birthday Parties were when the soda had fizzled and the partygoers had pooped out?

Yes, Lord, thank You for the chance to give my siblings what I'm sure is a much-needed break from their parenting responsibilities.

Just as we drove up, Pete stepped out the front door and helped unload the kids. Pete is my diesel mechanic brother. He's so big, he doesn't even need hydraulics to lift the trucks. I'm sure of that, because when he hugs me, I get squeezed down a size smaller. I love getting squeezed by Pete.

After the size-changing squeeze, he stepped behind me and said—and I love this part: "Close your eyes now." And he put his hands over my eyes and led me into my mom's dining room, and then everyone said—and I love this part too: "Surprise!"

And then everything went black. Almost literally. No, it wasn't because Pete was squeezing me again. The streamers were black. The helium balloons attached to my Queen of Birthday Parties chair were black. The cake was black. And the plastic fountain thing that sprayed away from the largest "50" I had ever seen was black too. I had never imagined before that it was possible to find a black plastic fountain.

And there were all my family—those rotten siblings and nieces and nephews and my mom—singing "Happy Birthday to You" and showering me with birthday presents that would help me forever remember I had turned old enough to start receiving AARP mail and *Modern Maturity.* A box of fifty garbage bags, fifty Styrofoam plates, fifty breath mints, fifty packets of Equal, and about forty-six other such things, all in fifties, including fifty pennies. Oh, and who will ever forget the statuette of Harry S Truman. I was so grateful for that. I had never realized that Harry S Truman was president when I was born.

And I must say, officially, as the Queen of Birthday Parties, that it was a perfect fiftieth celebration. I was with the people I loved the most. I was spoiled royally. And there was a lot of black ... and I look good in black.

So, *thank You, Lord, for turning a Potential Pity Party into a happy-birthday-to-me celebration.*

Janet Holm McHenry (California) is a speaker and author of seventeen books, including *Prayer Walk, Daily Prayer Walk,* and *Prayer Changes Teens: How to Parent from Your Knees.* She is an English teacher and the mother of four. www.DailyPrayerwalking.com

"The Value of Family"

BY DIANE B. AVERILL

It was just after I turned fifty that my dad died. Diagnosed on Father's Day with cancer, he was gone within six weeks. That event shook me like no other in my life. I had lost other family members before. My grandmother died when I was eighteen, and though I greatly grieved that loss, my whole life was still ahead of me. Now it was different. Suddenly I was faced with the fact that I would soon be in the oldest generation in my family. I had lost my dad, and I had to begin to deal with my own mortality as well. I had a new vantage point from which to see things. Overnight, time seemed more limited, and I began to think about what was most important in life.

As I thought about my life, it struck me that I had never felt unloved by my parents. I began to realize that this was an incredible gift. I recognized that what I had assumed was a normal feature growing up was, in reality, unique. I began to consider why relationships were so important in my family.

My parents were part of what has been described the "greatest generation." They fell in love and married just before World War II. They were first-generation Americans, born of immigrant stock. Growing up in the Depression, my parents knew what it felt like to be hungry. My mom once told me that she knew very early on that there was no Santa Claus. Given the poverty of her family, he was the only one who could bring her the simple presents she wanted. He never delivered any.

However, in the midst of deprivation, there was lots of love. When my dad enlisted in the Army Air Corps, my mother followed him around the country from military base to military base. Sometimes, the only contact they could have was holding hands at the base chapel when he had a brief amount of leave. As hard as this was, they wanted to be together as much as possible before my dad went overseas.

Their first years of marriage were marred by tragedy, including the death of my dad's sister, my mother's father, and one of their closest army friends. My dad's army experience included eighteen months in a prisoner of war camp. His plane was shot down over Germany only one day after he heard about my sister's birth. For almost three months, my mother, having given birth two months prematurely, had only the slimmest bit of hope that my dad was still alive. Crewmembers from other aircraft had counted parachutes coming out of my dad's B-17 as it fell to earth. Since only two of the entire crew remained on board and were presumed dead, at least the odds were in my dad's favor. On Good Friday, 1944, my mother received the news that he was a prisoner of war, and most important, that he was alive.

It was only after five decades that I began to wonder how they managed to get through those difficult times. My life had been so easy in comparison. I began to think about the fact that with all the major traumas they experienced, my parents never went to a counselor, never took a tranquilizer, and never let those tragedies in life limit their wholeness either as a married couple or as parents. They simply put it all behind them and went on.

What made them, and for that matter, many from their generation, so different? I believe it was the value placed on relationships. In a culture that often had little material goods, family was most important. There was a real sense of community, because everyone had to work together. Extended family members lived close by, and often multiple generations lived under one roof. There was support for my mom while my dad was overseas. Every day my grandfather took two streetcars to the hospital, carrying breast milk for his premature granddaughter. At night, my grandmother took turns walking a crying baby so my mom could sleep. Family and community worked together to provide emotional, financial, and spiritual support.

In addition, the limitation of material possessions was better understood. I remember breaking something and hearing my mom say, "Oh, it's only a thing." People were always more important than material objects. Living through deprivation helped them know that happiness could be found in the simple pleasures of life. Today we say that people are most important, but I often wonder if this is true considering the time we spend acquiring and maintaining things.

Faith also played a major role in my parents' lives and the community at large. My parents lived out what they believed, and they passed it on to their children. Because of a strong trust in God, they could be generous with their time and money. Sacrifice seemed to come naturally. Even as my dad lay in bed, gravely ill, he still was concerned that his grandchildren were given money so they could go play miniature golf. Even while dying, he was thinking of them.

The day after his death, my mother went through all his well-organized legal documents and found a letter he had written to her. He addressed it, "Dear Gorgeous," and went on to say that if she was reading the letter he had preceded her in death. He listed all the things he loved about her and stated that he just wanted one more time to tell her he loved her.

The importance of relationships was the theme that played throughout my parents' life. A faith in God, through Christ, provided a framework for it all. Strength beyond themselves got them through the tough times and provided the power to make the future better. It gave them a perspective to value people above possessions and a hope for an eternal future. Fifty years later, I am the grateful beneficiary of that perspective.

Diane B. Averill (New Hampshire) is a speaker and writer who has been married to her minister husband, Brent, for thirty-five years. They have four adult children and two sons-in-law. Diane has co-authored Bible studies and other outreach materials. Averillfam@rcn.net

Truth Four:

Freedom Is Found in Simplicity

"Too Much"

BY LUCINDA SECREST McDOWELL

I knew I was in trouble the minute I opened the door to my small closet. How? The huge pile at the bottom was my first clue. Somehow during the night the weight of all my hanging clothes won a battle with the ancient rod, and it snapped in two, spilling everything to the floor. What a mess!

Overload. Too many clothes, too little space. As I dug through the jumble, I discovered garments I had long forgotten. In fact, some led me to wonder why I had ever bought them in the first place. Clearly it was time to sort and simplify. While filling bags and bags of stuff for the church thrift shop, I realized that my whole life was a lot like my closet. Too much stuff, too little time. I suspected that some sort of impending collapse would soon force me to simplify my schedule.

Ann Morrow Lindbergh discovered this truth fifty years ago when she penned these words in *Gift from the Sea*:

> My life in Connecticut, I begin to realize, lacks this quality of significance and therefore of beauty, because there is so little empty space. The space is scribbled on; the time has been filled. There are so few empty pages in my

engagement pad, or empty hours in the day or empty rooms in my life in which to stand alone and find myself. Too many activities and people and things. Too many worthy activities, valuable things and interesting people. For it is not merely the trivial which clutters our lives but the important as well. We can have a surfeit of treasures—an excess of shells—where one or two would be significant.

I am finally beginning to understand the concept of Less Is More.

Like many in my baby-boomer generation, my sisters and I have recently been helping our elderly parents to make the transition from their home into a retirement community. And after fifty-five years of marriage, three children, and nine grandchildren, and only three moves, my folks had a lot of stuff! Needless to say, when my sisters and I were sorting and dividing it, we became quite overwhelmed. I vowed right then that I would begin to downsize long before I reached that stage of life.

I decided to begin by streamlining my closet. In fact, now everything in it is gone. Due to losing quite a bit of weight, I now have the gift of starting over in a smaller size. I am content with a couple of jackets and pants and several skirts, blouses, and sweaters. It makes my life so much easier that I wonder why I didn't simplify long ago. I am still working on streamlining my schedule, but I have definitely learned to say no.

There is great freedom to be found when we decide what is most important and then relegate everything else to the pile marked "optional." My summer project is to purge the basement of our parsonage. After thirteen years and four children, it's stuffed. Since this was also my summer project for the past two years (and obviously didn't get done), you have permission to check up on me. Please.

Lucinda Secrest McDowell, M.T.S. (Connecticut) presents "Encouraging Words that Transform" through her international conference speaking and writing. A graduate of Gordon-Conwell Seminary, she is the author of five books including *Quilts from Heaven, Women's Spiritual Passages,* and *Amazed by Grace.* www.EncouragingWords.net

"The Second Half of the Ride"

BY MARTHA BOLTON

I remember as a child going to carnivals and amusement parks with my family. After waiting in long lines, some for nearly an hour, I'd climb onto the ride with so much excitement I could barely contain myself.

About halfway through the ride, though, my focus would change. Instead of enjoying the remainder of the ride, I could hardly wait for it to be over so I could rush back to the end of the line and ride it again.

I rarely paid much attention to the second half. All I could think about was how much fun it was going to be the next time around. Or the third time. Or the fourth.

I'm sure I missed out on a lot of fun during the second half of those rides. Those who design amusement parks don't put all the thrills in the first half of a ride. They usually design them to be an exciting experience from start to finish. In fact, the second half is often the best part of the ride. The fun is there to be enjoyed. If we're not paying attention, there's no one to blame but ourselves.

Life can be like an amusement park ride. It can be a series of gently paced ups and downs like a merry-go-round, or it can be a roller-coaster adventure from start to finish with lots of exhilarating highs and breathtaking lows. Wherever the ride takes us or how much we choose to enjoy it, one thing is for certain: There is no second go-around. We can't hop off this ride and run to the back of the line and do it again. We only get one ticket. When our ride in this world is over, that's it—for this portion of the adventure anyway.

Chances are you're at the halfway point of the ride. Barring accidents, many, if not most of us, will live to be seventy or eighty or beyond. That means we've got almost as many years left to live as we've already lived. So we shouldn't rush through it. If we close our eyes during the second half of this ride, we might be missing out on what could very well be the very best part.

A lot of what we allow to consume our time and energy isn't really important, at least not in the big picture. So just in case we ever question whether or not something is worth all the attention we're giving it, the following chart is provided:

PRIORITIES

Worth Our Time	*Not Worth Our Time*
A good book	A TV show with no redeeming qualities
Thankfulness	Selfishness
Appreciating others	Petty jealousies
Friends who stand by you	Friends who desert you
Helping others	Getting even with others
Encouraging people	Discouraging people
Spending time with family	Working unnecessary overtime
Taking a long walk	Waiting in long lines
Having a pet	Fretting over a neighbor's pet
Love	Hate
Striving for excellence	Striving to bury your competition
Peace of mind	Worry over things you can't control

Martha Bolton (Tennessee), former comedy writer for Bob Hope, is the author of more than forty books which include children's entertainment, youth devotionals, musicals, comedy essays, dramatic sketches, and works on marriage, family, and relationships. Her mission statement: "Life's tough. God's good. And laughter is calorie free!" www.MarthaBolton.com

"Enough Is Enough"

BY LUCI SWINDOLL

A few years ago a friend was spending the weekend with me, and when we awakened on Saturday morning she asked, "What shall we do today? Where would it be fun to go? The mall? The movies? The museum?" I think she was pretty stunned when I suggested we stay home. "And do *what*?" she questioned. "Shouldn't we go someplace? It's Saturday!"

I said, "Why don't we do something here and enjoy what we already have?"

"Oh," she muttered. But she became intrigued with the idea as I explained how I feel that we sometimes go running around looking for and buying more things—things we might already have. Why don't we just stay at home and enjoy them?

That's what my friend and I did that day ... *and she loved it*. We worked a jigsaw puzzle, listened to our favorite music, read to each other, played a game, made little meals, all the while having wonderful conversation. We went to bed that night completely satisfied.

Since that day my friend has said to me many times, "That helped me so much. I've learned to stay home and enjoy what I already have." Now when she comes here she never wants to leave.

What we learned that day is that enough is enough, even though there are times we're afraid to test it. We're kind of scared that what we have won't be enough to satisfy us.

"I have learned the secret of being content in any and every situation, whether well fed or hungry, whether living in plenty or in want" (Phil. 4:12).

Luci Swindoll (California) is on her successful third career as a speaker for Women of Faith and an author of books such as *I Married Adventure, Wide My World, Narrow My Bed,* and *You Bring the Confetti.* www.WomenOfFaith.com

"Simple Joy"

I was playing "Coupon Queen" at the grocery store checkout when a new magazine lured me with its stunning photo of a white terry robe, red flowers in its pocket, and a promise of an article about simpler living. Normally I ignore the literature stacked above the gum and candy—except for laughing over reports of a space alien baby in Kalamazoo or that eating peanut butter will give me washboard abs. But the clerk was too lightning-fingered for me to scan the magazine for free while waiting. Overcome by irrationality, I tossed it on the conveyer belt—and there went my coupon savings of the day.

My "frugalholic" conscience chided me as I got home and browsed through the magazine's full-page ads for makeup, brand-name clothes, and convenience foods. Its "simple living" article suggested paring down one's social life. No problem here. My social life climaxes at attending my teens' orchestra concerts and stopping for an ice cream cone afterwards.

When I was my teens' age, I wondered what I would be at fifty. Now I know. Whatever standards of material success I once held, I now find myself adjusting in the opposite direction in search of simple joys. Stretching a teacher's pension has something to do with it. Heritage has another.

After my parents' deaths, I found the ledger book they kept in their first year of marriage in 1941. It recorded buying milk, 38 cents; a meal out, 50 cents; and a month's rent, $61.77. Most months they budgeted to within a dollar. January had a deficit of $1.46 from an income of $108.74. Here and there I noticed a figure for "personal allowance." "Mad money," they used to call it.

Eventually, their financial circumstances improved. They put two daughters through college, paid off a modest home, and took a few overseas "dream" trips. Then Mom's cancer consumed their savings. My mother died at fifty-nine, and Dad died six months later, of a heart attack.

They were teenagers during the Depression, and as I cleaned out their home I discovered how much those early fears of "not having enough" carried to adulthood. Clothing crammed three closets. Plastic bags, stuffed with more plastic bags, were pinned to a clothesline in the furnace room. A canning closet hid jars of food too old to eat safely. Yardage spilled from the linen closet. A high kitchen cupboard yielded dozens of salt-and-pepper shakers, for which there was no collection display space.

Since then, I have helped with the cleanout after four more deaths—each with its telltale piles of hoarding. And each time, I am forced to ask myself what people will say when they pick through *my* stuff. The question becomes more poignant as I consider how a drinking driver nearly ended my life at fifty, and how I am now almost the age my mother was when she died.

Whoever picks through my things, I hope they will remember someone who sought to follow five disciplines of simplicity.

First was to **save up,** not to amass riches but to reduce debt. Isaiah 5:8 denounces materialism and those who "add house to house and join field to field till no space is left." The great

Methodist evangelist John Wesley once commented that he earned all he could, to save all he could, to give all he could. In other words, by living frugally and simply, he could release more funds for God's work. My husband and I scrimped on a teacher's salary (including my coupon efforts) to pay off our house mortgage early, saving more than $50,000 in interest. Doing so enabled us to help friends in seminary and mission work, support two children in compassion ministries, and give to other needs. One time our Africa child, son of a pastor killed in that nation's genocide, wrote how our extra support money enabled his family to buy food and sit down for a meal together. "That really gripped me," my husband said after our own simple family meal from which we had leftovers.

Second, to **free up** unused possessions by surrendering ownership to God. Missionary statesman Hudson Taylor annually sorted through all his belongings, giving away what he hadn't used for a year. He believed God would hold him accountable for anything he retained and didn't use, when others could use it. I am not quite there yet, but I do try to keep that standard before me as I ask what I truly need and sort out for yard sales or giveaways.

Third and fourth, to **use up** and **fix up** to avoid waste. When I sewed our patchwork quilts from others' sewing scraps, I turned trash into beauty. We found many of our furnishings at yard sales and thrift stores; repaired or repainted, they function well. My home won't make the pages of a beautiful-house magazine, but it offers a sense of peace and order to my family. We have our share of hand-me-down clothes, but they are mended and clean.

Fifth, to **look up,** to seek enjoyment in God's creative gifts. One is music, whether it's a high school concert or a symphony resurrected from a piece of plastic via an inherited stereo system. It's a tangerine and flamingo sunrise chalked across the skyline while I spoon in hot oatmeal with chunks of apples. It's bread baking and Crock-Pot turkey soup simmering. It's biting into taut purple grapes and crunchy green bell peppers and letting the flavors linger on my tongue.

It's looking out the kitchen window at quail strutting, like come-alive Egyptian paintings, over to the clearance-sale birdbath beneath mammoth blue spruce that began as seedlings twenty years earlier. It's that "how-are-you" call from a friend, babies' powder-sweet smiles, cats purring, sun shafts through the storm clouds, twenty-minute naps that chase headaches, clean windows, earth's perfume after a summer rain, and good shoes for morning walks.

And most important, it's being quiet before God—the lyrics of beloved hymns running through my heart, the sun on my back as I read my Bible, and the privilege of praying to the Father-Creator who originated ... simple joy.

Jeanne Zornes (Washington) is a conference speaker and award-winning author. She has had nearly a thousand articles and short stories published along with seven books, including *When I Felt Like Ragweed, God Saw a Rose.* zornesj@crcwnet.com

"The Silence Speaks"

BY GLORIA GAITHER

Stillness is more audible than any sound, not tinny like so many sounds I hear these days.

The silence is full and rich, insistent ... demanding that I listen and suggesting always that I'd be foolish not to. Only fools refuse the counsel of the wise, and this silence seems to know everything. It seems I've been a prodigal, traipsing along behind the band just like a thoughtless gypsy anywhere the living was easy, stealing morsels when I could have had the loaf.

Maybe it's the oaks and beeches. These oaks have housed a thousand generations of owls and jays, and have withstood abuse from countless woodpeckers and men. They've seen the fleet-footed native children tossing pebbles at their roots and chasing little fawns around between them. They've stood and heard the council casting lots for war or peace while fragrant pipe smoke wafted through their branches.

Perhaps it is the brook, whispering of its secret travels, nurturing the earth along its way, or maybe it's the earth, the pregnant fertile earth, pulling me like influential kin back to my moorings and my heritage.

The earth is calling me home to the simple and eternal things.

It persistently calls me to reject the glitter of the transient and return to the Father's house.

The silence—a voice asking one pointed and unavoidable question: Will I return and inherit the earth? And here in the silence, the only sound to be heard is the whisper of my own answer.

Gloria Gaither (Indiana) is a songwriter, speaker, and music artist who enjoys Homecoming ministry with her husband, Bill Gaither. Their union has produced more than six hundred songs, sixty recordings, numerous awards, a dozen musicals, a collection of books, three children, and four grandchildren. www.Gaithernet.com

"Simply Go Lightly"

BY FRAN CAFFEY SANDIN

Years ago my husband, Jim, and I eagerly anticipated our ten-day trip to London for a medical conference. It couldn't have been more exciting, like a dream come true. The only problem occurred when I began packing my huge suitcase—the unsinkable Molly Brown.

Of course I wanted to cover all the possible scenarios with the fall weather, plus I frequently changed my mind about what to wear. So I included various colored shoes, raincoats, gloves, dresses, skirts, blouses, and pants outfits. Then as a nurse I wanted to take care of any health matters that might arise for the entire group. After covering all the contingency plans—hot packs, cold packs, pills, and powders—I concluded that everything was complete short of the bedpan—and it just wouldn't fit.

When departure time came, I literally sat on old Molly while Jim struggled to close the latches. Sweat beaded on his forehead as he moaned, "What do you have in here anyway? Bricks?"

"Well, Jim," I explained sweetly, "you know how far from home we'll be, and you never know what we might need."

Old Molly's sides were bulging when Jim finally heaved her from the bed onto the floor, and I proudly announced, "Look, Jim, I got everything into *one* suitcase."

With a pained expression, my long-suffering hubby placed one hand on his aching back and declared, "That's amazing."

We whirled off to Europe, and old Molly held together until the last day when I braced myself to pick her up in the airport, and she didn't budge. There I stood holding only the handle. It was beyond repair, so Jim and I took turns shoving her to the car. The two-ton, unsinkable Molly Brown had finally sunk.

As I mused about our trip, the delightful memories were sprinkled with nagging reminders of all the time I had wasted packing, unpacking, and repacking the unnecessary stuff we never used. So on future trips, I concentrated on shortening my list.

It seemed a miracle in the nineties when I traveled for two weeks in Norway with only two carry-on bags. (Jim took one well-designed carry-on with zippered sections as we attended an International Christian Medical Society meeting.) I loved the small bags as we used various modes of travel—train, ship, bus, and plane—and sometimes we ran, carrying everything, through the terminals to make our connections.

Now that I have learned to travel more simply, I can joyfully share some of my favorite travel tips:

Choose from an array of knits and wrinkle-free clothing.

Decide on a basic color (either black or navy works well). Mix and match brighter colored blouses and scarves, but take only one pair of comfortable flats, one pair of heels, and one pair of walking shoes for your entire trip. Try different combinations as you pack, and include accessories as needed.

When traveling to a cold climate, pack long, silk underwear for extra warmth.

Layer clothing off and on for comfort. I never travel anytime without a light sweater or jacket.

Keep a makeup kit ready to go. I use mine every day so I know it has everything.

Replenish your toiletry travel kit when you get home so it is ready for the next trip. Take disposable washcloths for makeup removal.

Place tissue paper between layers of dress clothes to minimize wrinkling, and pack dresses in plastic cleaner's bags.

Use self-closure bags for some items, and squeeze the air out to maximize space.

Keep vitamins, medications, etc., in a plastic case, ready to go.

Pack a soft nylon duffle bag to use for day trips and for bringing home gifts.

Take only the cards and documents you need, use a mini-wallet, and carry a featherweight purse.

Traveling light requires more planning time, but is definitely more carefree and fun. Now I check out the activities planned and select a few appropriate items. Then I pack and go. If it won't fit in my small rolling bag and tote, I don't take it. If I forget something, I either do without it or buy a substitute.

After fifty years, God has taught me something about being lighthearted in my daily spiritual walk as well. In the past, I have lugged around my "spiritual suitcase" loaded with bricks of regret, all the while looking in the rearview mirror instead of at the road ahead. I once read a little sign: "Never let too much of yesterday take up too much of today." That has been a problem for me as too often

I have allowed my thoughts to be cluttered with the heaviness of past sins and mistakes.

Then one day I read the words of a pastor: "When we concentrate on our failings instead of the Lord's power and grace to free us from the guilt of having failed, we're helping Satan. After all, as long as we're beating ourselves up, he doesn't have to!"

Ouch. I knew I didn't want to be on Satan's side. These verses reminded me of God's forgiveness: "The LORD is compassionate and gracious, slow to anger and abounding in lovingkindness. ... As far as the east is from the west, so far has He removed our transgressions from us" (Ps. 103:8, 12 NASB). Claiming God's sacrificial love for me through Christ, I tossed out that brick of guilt. Because He has forgiven me, *I can forgive myself* and look ahead with much more strength, energy, and confidence.

Then there were bricks of pride and selfishness. It has taken the Lord many years to help me unpack that junk and replace it with trusting love for Him and genuine concern for others. It is a lifelong process, but Jesus invites the weary and heavy-laden to grasp the truth of His *unsinkable* love for each of us. We can traverse the road of our lives and travel lightly because He has promised, "My yoke is easy, and My load is light" (Matt. 11:30 NASB).

Fran Caffey Sandin (Texas) has authored *Touching the Clouds, Encouraging Stories to Make Your Faith Soar,* and *See You Later, Jeffrey,* and contributed to ten other books. A nurse, organist, speaker, and grandmother, she lives in Greenville, Texas. www.FranSandin.com

"Simplicity"

BY MARY WHELCHEL

A wise saying states, "Someday, the things we own may end up owning us." It is easy to allow the accumulation of "stuff"—things we think we can't live without—to complicate our lives needlessly. Possessions meant to simplify our daily routine end up weighing us down as we spend time, energy, emotion, and money in maintaining them.

A friend of mine went to a foreign country for a two-year missionary assignment. At the end of her term, before returning home, she gave away everything she had accumulated while there, so all that remained fit onto one shelf in her closet. She wrote me and said, "I can't tell you how freeing it is to know that all my earthly possessions can fit onto just one shelf. It makes life so simple."

I, too, felt the need to simplify my life by selling my home in order to find a smaller townhouse that was easier to maintain. While I loved my house and had enjoyed decorating it, living in a townhouse has eliminated many unnecessary responsibilities. I realize that *where* I live is not nearly as important as *how* I live.

Jesus warned, "Be on your guard against all kinds of greed; a man's life does not consist in the abundance of his possessions" (Luke 12:15). When we hold onto possessions, considering them *treasures*, we come dangerously close to being greedy. I have discovered that the key to abundant living is in holding onto the only *true treasure*, Jesus Christ Himself. Because I have Him, I have everything!

Mary Whelchel (Illinois) is a national conference speaker and the founder of the Christian Working Woman radio broadcast in Chicago. Her books include *Quiet Moments for Working Women, Getting Along with People @ Work,* and *The Christian Working Woman.* www.ChristianWorkingWoman.org

TRUTH FIVE:

Pain Either Destroys or Transforms

"No Struggle, No Soaring"

BY LUCINDA SECREST MCDOWELL

As another crying child ran back to her parents' pew, I knew she was genuinely frightened, but I didn't know what to do. So I continued presenting the children's sermon, while silently praying for everyone involved.

Every Sunday morning the children would stream down the aisles toward the front of the sanctuary for their special time in the church service. Being a college community, we had lots of children, many from faculty like my husband, who was Dean of Students. While I knew all the regulars, we also had guests almost every Sunday, as Montreat was also a popular retreat center.

And it was the children of the guests who weren't prepared when they saw Joel, the son of our biology professor. At age ten, Joel had already had scores of surgeries on his body, and the scars covered him from head to toe. When he was only two years old, his family's car was hit by a trailer truck and burst into flames. By the time little Joel was rescued, he had been burned over 88 percent of his body. Not only had he lost a hand, but his face had to be rebuilt. Onlookers were often cruel.

While his physical appearance both attracted and repelled people, those who knew Joel's spirit and personality could not help but be impressed. He had a zest for life and a determination to conquer and thrive despite his limitations. With the help of his godly and supportive parents, Mike and Janet Sonnenberg, Joel decided that his pain would not destroy, but transform.

By the time he entered high school he was captain of the soccer team, president of the student body, and prince of the junior prom. Later, at Taylor University he was elected president of the sophomore class. Recently Joel appeared on the CBS program *48 Hours* and revealed his secret: "If I did not believe in God, then I'm doing all this pain for nothing. If I did not believe in God, then all these surgeries that I have gone through and continue to go through is for nothing."

But perhaps one of his greatest tests was when the truck driver who caused the accident was found, arrested, and brought to justice *nineteen years after the accident.* In court Joel Sonnenberg faced the man who had changed his life forever with these words: "This is my prayer for you that you may know that grace has no limits. We will not consume our lives with hatred because hatred brings only misery. Yet we will surround our lives with love, unconditional love in God's grace."

I can't imagine what it must be like to endure pain as Joel has done, but I know that the quality of his life today is due to his choice to live through the process. I am reminded of the caterpillar, which goes through a death-like period of inactivity while in its cocoon. All is dark and unproductive. It seems as though the end has come, and there is no hope. But there is more, thanks to the Creator of the universe.

As this creature struggles to break through the chrysalis, its body emits a secretion that enables it to emerge as a beautiful butterfly and soar into the sky. Unfortunately, without the struggle to escape the cocoon, the secretions would not be released and the creature could never fly.

Pain is part of all our lives, but we often want to fast-forward to the soaring part and miss the struggle. This is not how God created us. May we embrace the pain and let it transform us into stronger women of purpose and power. So that, like Joel, we may know in our hearts that grace has no limits.

Lucinda Secrest McDowell, M.T.S. (Connecticut) presents "Encouraging Words that Transform" through her international conference speaking and writing. A graduate of Gordon-Conwell Seminary, she is the author of five books including *Quilts from Heaven, Women's Spiritual Passages,* and *Amazed by Grace.* www.EncouragingWords.net

"Mending Broken Hearts"

BY PATSY CLAIRMONT

Somehow I thought by my age anything broken inside me would be fixed. Instead, I'm learning that healing and journey are synonymous, and that as long as there is breath in my body there will also be something that needs mending. It's the human condition. That makes sense to me because for a long time I looked for people who had pulled their acts together, but I kept finding other fractured folks who, like me, were in need of repair.

So am I suggesting that all we can hope for in this life is a slightly improved version of our original design? Perhaps. I guess it depends on what kind of effort and dedication we're willing to put into the journey.

God is a God of grace, and He doesn't want us frantically striving to know Him. Yet He does want a relationship with us, which means we have to do more than show up. We can do nothing to qualify—Christ did that on our behalf—but we can be responsive to who He is and what He asks of us.

We can respond to God by, first, **sitting down.** That I can do. And when you think about it, that's all Jesus asks of us—what we can do. Begin wherever you are and take the next obvious step in your journey.

Second, **we need to weep**. Not all tears are from sadness; some are from pure joy. Like hearing the sound of your mother's voice or hearing God speak your name. Don't resist authentic emotions. They are designed that we might feel life and express a myriad of sentiments, including sadness and joy.

Third, **we need to mourn**. Even though we all must mourn our losses, grieving does have an end. It is a season, not a permanent lodging; you won't have to have your mail sent there. The loss may always be with you, but the pain eases. Honest.

Fourth, **we must fast**. Giving up is often the first step in growing up. Denial isn't natural, but it's important to the vitality of our existence. Otherwise we risk becoming self-indulgent dolts.

Fifth, **we must pray**. Imagine us, on speaking terms with the Lord. He is the only One I know with shoulders broad enough to carry all that weighs me down. And kneeling down in His presence lifts me up. Perhaps that's why we're instructed to pray without ceasing. The Lord *always* has our best interest in mind.

And that's good reason to celebrate. Speaking of which, another part of mending our hearts is relearning how to enter jubilation.

Patsy Clairmont (Michigan) is a dynamic speaker for Women of Faith and has authored many books such as *God Uses Cracked Pots, Normal Is Just a Setting on Your Dryer, Mending Your Heart in a Broken World,* and *Tea with Patsy Clairmont.* www.PatsyClairmont.com

"Perfect Peace for Parents of Prodigals"

BY JUDY HAMPTON

There came a day in my life when I cried out to God, "For this I have stretch marks?"

Through tears I reasoned: "Lord, I am worn out trying to live my life with a prodigal son. It's too painful, Lord, it's too hard. I feel like such a failure. How can I rewrite the past? If I had parenting to do all over, I'd do it so differently, but now it's too late. Oh Lord, I simply cannot go on."

For fifteen years, my husband and I wrestled with the heartache of a wayward son. He began wandering into the pigpen of life when he was a senior in high school. My husband had been transferred to Denver, Colorado, and our son stayed behind in California to finish out his last year of school. He was going to live with an awesome host family from our church. But in time, problems arose.

We were shocked. Outside of normal adolescent behavior, we had experienced few real problems with him.

"I'll handle everything," my husband explained in full confidence to the host family. But he soon learned that we couldn't handle much of anything.

Our son is a bright guy—a gifted athlete with a sense of humor that is unparalleled. When he put his mind to something, he always succeeded. And he enjoyed years of popularity and success. But what he wasn't counting on was sin: mind-altering drugs. His choices would take him down a long and lonely road toward a dead end.

He would occasionally experience periods of sobriety. But when the pressures of life mounted, he would escape back into drug use. The results were always the same: job losses, financial struggles, and despair.

Being the typical American parents, we rescued him whenever he called. "We'll just help him this one time," my husband assured me. "Just until he gets on his feet. I think he's finally learned his lesson." Little did we know how much our rescuing was hindering rather than helping.

In one of his sober periods of life, he met and married an adorable girl. They pursued the good life. They had three babies in two years, because they had twins. As the pressures of life closed in once again, money became extremely tight, and he ran back to that comfort of substance abuse. Their marriage spiraled into an abyss. They sought the counsel of the culture and were told that all his problems were because of us! We hadn't parented him correctly, and he did not feel loved.

"What? What do you mean? We did the best job we knew how. Is this the thanks we get for all the sacrifices we've made?" we defended. The litany of rationalization and anger escalated until we were told that we could no longer see our grandchildren.

"Oh my God! Oh my God!" I screamed in disbelief when my husband shared the news.

"Our grandchildren? The ones we've adored and cared for and nurtured and loved? Why? Why? Why are we being punished? Why are the grandchildren being punished?" I sobbed.

But the verdict was in, and we were out.

I couldn't sleep at night. I wandered the darkened house crying uncontrollably, begging God to help us. I worried about the demise of my son's life in Christ. In the daytime, I ran to everyone for advice, but I seldom ran to God. But one day in desperation I fell to my knees.

"Oh God, please forgive me for worrying so much, for not trusting You. Please forgive me for my spiritual laziness and my lackluster prayer life—and for the sin of unbelief. I have believed a lie about Your not being sovereign. Oh God, thank You for allowing all of this. Lord, change me. Change me!"

And that day I made a decision to get serious about my relationship with God. I had been a Christian for years, but I lacked the discipline to meet with the Lord daily. As I began reading His Word, I began to develop a prayer life.

As He renewed my mind, I tapped into His transforming power. I took Paul's counsel in Philippians 4:6 (NASB): "Be anxious for nothing, but in everything by prayer and supplication with thanksgiving let your requests be made known to God."

And one day I laid it all down before Him. My pain was so deep, but I found God to be so big. "Lord, I surrender our son to You. And our grandchildren. And all my sins, and mistakes as a mom. Father, I surrender everything into Your capable hands. Please forgive me for counting on them for my life, instead of counting on You. I see from Your Word that You are everything I need. You are my God, and my King, my Provider, and the Sustainer of all things. If our son is never restored to us, I know I can trust You with him. Have Your way with him."

And in that place of utter surrender, His Living Grace provided me with the peace that passes all understanding (see Phil. 4:7 KJV). My husband noticed an immediate change in me.

You see, I had learned the secret of the Christian life. And I learned it on my fifieth birthday: Christ in me, the hope of glory (see Col. 1:27). I found Him to be sufficient for all circumstances.

In time our son came to saving faith in Jesus Christ. So did his wife. Their conversions were absolutely dramatic. God began to resurrect their lives and make them something far more beautiful than I had ever dreamed. Today our son is a pastor in a thriving church with a passion for the gospel.

Looking back, I see how God used this painful time to transform me. In time, it transformed my husband as well.

I can say with confidence that it was the sweetest time in our lives.

Judy Hampton (California) is a Christian author and keynote speaker for women's conferences in the United States and internationally. She has appeared on *Focus on the Family, Decision Today,* and other Christian television programs. www.JudyHampton.com

"Restoration"

BY JAN KARON

I found it at a favorite antique shop. It had come all the way from France and was very old. I loved it at once. It was a lamp. This little lamp, whose base was the hand-painted porcelain figure of a yellow bird, came home with me and sat on my mantle. When I switched on the light, ... I always thought the little bird might sing. It was very delicate and lifelike, my favorite lamp in a lifetime of lamps.

A tile-setter was working in my house, and repositioned a chair so that the lamp cord went round the chair leg. When I moved the chair, unknowing, the lamp smashed onto the floor. I remember standing over it, frozen and unbelieving. ... There were twelve fragments of porcelain, some very small. I put them in a box, chiding myself for being so fond of a created thing. I thought the little lamp was gone forever. But not so. ... I discovered a one-hundred-year-old family-owned restoration company in Philadelphia. They said many of their restorations are nearly impossible to detect ...

Last week my little bird returned to her perch on the mantle. And, needless to say, these human eyes can't detect where the breaks occurred.

The lamp reminds me daily how God is able to lovingly restore us through His Son. All we have to do is ask for restoration, for healing, for new life. Christ was sent that we may be restored. When we offer Him a willing and contrite heart, we have only to ask, and He will make us brand-new.

Jan Karon (Virginia) is the author of the very popular Mitford series which began with *At Home in Mitford* and has continued for eight books through her latest release *Shepherds Abiding*. She has also written eight other gift books. www.MitfordBooks.com

"Running Partners"

BY RUTH C. LEE

For a long time my sleep has been disturbed, restless, and drugged with dreams. One dream in particular plagues the late-night hour—a dream about running a race. Even though I like to run, I am quite slow and sloppy. I try not to run on busy roads because I can only imagine what I look like. I run now almost as an act of worship. At fifty, the aches and pains accompany me, so I slowly and deliberately put one foot in front of the other one—God and me, laces tied, running the race. And though I have never actually run in a road race, this particular dream began a few years ago and stays with me even now.

It is the day of a marathon road race. There are people lining both sides of the road, and the starting line is decorated with yellow banners. Many runners, including me, are excitedly stepping up to the starting line, ready, prepared, willing themselves to run the race. But, something or someone is missing. Even though my running clothes are fitted properly, and my race number is pinned to my T-shirt, I am somewhat frantically looking at the crowd. I seem to be desperately trying to find someone, and I feel myself starting to panic, to sweat.

Just as I glance at the starting official, he fires the starter's pistol.

In one huge mass first step, the runners lunge forward, straining ahead, and begin to run. I, too, lean forward, looking straight ahead, and signal my body to run. But I do not run. I do not even move. Everyone passes me. Everyone. When I look down, I discover to my horror that I have no legs. No legs. It is graphic and frightening, and I always wake up at this point. Dozens of times, I fall at the starting line.

During a counseling session, after I had shared this dream that kept haunting me, the psychologist said to my husband, "You're the legs. She's ready to run the race. She's looking for you."

I never got my legs.

Now, several years later, the dream returns with less frequency, though I still run—slow and sloppy and now single. Quietly, amazingly, humbly, I now look down and see new legs are growing. The old ones are gone, it is true. But, new ones are being created even while I am still wobbly and weak. The sheer unsteadiness and uncertainty is enough to keep me off the road many days. But, these new legs are meant to run. I don't particularly like to run single, and I definitely do not like the bends in the road of this race. Uphill, downhill, storms and burning heat, paralyzing cold, blistered feet, battered knees, and a weak heart refuse to choose a new companion.

I do run single, but I do not run alone. My Running Partner commands me to the starting line, just as He called Peter out of the boat: "Come. Strap on your shoes. Lace them with the cord of hope." Then He adds: "Strengthen your feeble arms and weak knees" (Heb. 12:12). He has even promised to "broaden the path beneath me, so that my ankles do not turn" (Ps. 18:36).

At fifty, the old roads still beckon seductively while new roads terrify. It is clear that I did not grow these new legs—I couldn't have; I don't have that kind of power. But Jehovah Rapha, "the LORD, who heals you" (Ex. 15:26), does have resurrection power right here on my front doorstep. And He provides the deep healing of wounds so that where stubs should have been, new legs surely grow.

My Partner stands ready. He is not slow or sloppy, nor does He run ahead and leave me in His dust. The bends in the road do not take Him by surprise or frighten Him. He doesn't seem to care that I am often wobbly and trip on the smallest pebble. We run the race set before us, and there are clouds of witnesses (see Heb. 12:1). Perhaps, many who thought they would never run again.

At the most crippling time of my life, when it seemed enough to retreat to my sickbed and sip the cup of sympathy and sorrow, Hope burst in, wrestled me from my pain, and announced a new race. "I have no legs!" I shouted. "Not to worry," Hope replied. "We never call anyone to run the race without perfectly equipping them. Your new legs will be there when the gun goes off. You'll look down, and what once was lost will most certainly be found."

> ... I remember my affliction and my wandering,
> the bitterness and the gall.
> I well remember them,
> and my soul is downcast within me.
> Yet this I call to mind
> and therefore I have hope:
> Because of the LORD's great love we are not consumed,
> for his compassions never fail,
> They are new every morning;
> great is your faithfulness.
>
> Lamentations 3:19–23

Ruth C. Lee (North Carolina) is on the staff of St. Mark's Church where she serves as pastor over women's ministries, singles, divorce recovery, and counseling. Her passion is developing a biblical recovery ministry. She is also a master storyteller.

"Still Picking Strawberries"

BY PATTI SELLERS BUBNA

Some months after my husband suddenly died, I traveled to Seattle to visit my youngest daughter, who was finishing college. Grief had disoriented and weakened us.

One Saturday we ventured into a pick-your-own strawberry field. We were seeking something tangible and earthy, and the intermingled smell of cultivated soil and ripened fruit brought solace to our stricken hearts.

Pails in hand, our knees wedged into the narrow ditches used for irrigation, Melanie and I set out to glean the berries. We had different agendas: hers was to find perfect berries, rejecting all others; mine was to strip off every berry that flashed mostly red. We were equally delighted in our quest, moving up and down the rows, our shoes growing heavy with an accumulation of dense clay.

In the distance, we could see one knot of pickers who had a little girl in tow. She meandered farther and farther away from her family. Eventually she wandered into earshot.

"Are you picking berries?" I asked.

She sidled up to me and shook her head. "I don't know how."

"Here, let me show you," I offered, lifting the leaves for her to see a cluster of strawberries. "Just look for a berry that is red all over.

You don't want one that is white on the end, or too mushy. Nice and firm. See? Give a little tug, and it will drop into your hand."

She looked at me with wonder. "*I* could pick a berry?"

"Sure," I invited. "It's lots of fun."

She bent her little body over the plants, a deep furrow of concentration on her face. "Is this a good berry?" she asked, pulling back the leaves for me to look.

"That's a good berry," I assured her, getting on with my own picking, enjoying each satisfying plunk into the pail. I could hear a little pop as she disconnected the fruit from its umbilical cord. There was silence for a few moments.

"And this one?" her little voice chirped. "Is this a good berry?" I nodded. "And this, is this a good berry?"

Beginning to grow weary of the questions and wanting her to feel confident in her own judgment, I asked, "What do *you* think?"

"*I* think it's a good berry," she answered soberly.

"Now you know how to pick berries," I assured her.

For long moments she hunched over the plants, her little bottom poked high into the air. With no pail or box in which to put her treasures, she clutched her chubby hands tightly around the fruit. Sticky ooze began to run down her arm.

"Don't squeeze so," I suggested. "Just pile your berries on top of one another or they will get squishy and drip juice everywhere. Maybe you should run back to your mama and put them in her pail."

She straightened up, patches of red smudge on her face. "How do you know so much about picking berries?" she asked.

"Oh, my mama taught me when I was about your age."

She stood, studying me for a few moments. Finally she spoke. "I guess by now you're so old you must know just about everything." With that pronouncement she toddled off.

I shook my head silently at her retreating figure. Never before had I felt so inept at deciphering what God was doing in my life. What did it all mean? This fresh pain, this new loss was forcing me to see God in a different way. He alternately seemed so insufferably obscure and so arrestingly distinct.

Certainly sorrow was not unique to me alone. By mid-age, few of us are unscathed by the brusque nature of grief. Some retreat. Others become cynical. But there is a wonderful contingent who blaze through the pain, ask the tough questions, reestablish their faith. You can spot them in a crowd—people whose eyes shine with just a hint of sadness. They carry themselves with confidence, grace, and dignity, no longer compelled to understand life's unanswerables. The crucible of pain has humbled and matured them.

More than anything, these folks have developed a contented spirit. The apostle Paul writes about it in his letter to the Philippians, chapter 4: "I have learned the secret of being content in any and every situation, whether well fed or hungry, whether living in plenty or in want" (v. 12).

Contentment is not an innate human talent; it takes practice. While it may look effortless on the surface, the hard work of trusting God is essential. Although contentment is internal and involves quietness of the heart, it is not a denial of emotions or pretending that everything is okay.

After one of the four memorial services for Paul, a man rushed up just as I was getting into the car. I recognized him as one of Paul's former parishioners and a licensed counselor. "Patti," he said to me with an air of authority, "Paul's death was not a tragedy." I wanted to scream, "Maybe not a tragedy for you!"

Maybe *you* didn't lose two spouses before you were fifty.

Maybe *you* didn't have your home and friendships and work snatched away.

Maybe *you* don't have children who are twice without a father.

It is difficult to reconcile that our discomfort and God's faithfulness can coexist. Contentment is a settled understanding that even grievous events fall within the bounds of His sovereignty.

I sometimes chafe at the idea of an empty house at the end of a long workday, and I am no stranger to loneliness. Life's realities can be so *disappointing*, and upheaval can be so *aggravating*. Still, none of these struggles debate God's faithfulness. He amply supplies joy for today and hope for tomorrow.

This is the secret of contentment.

Little girl, wait a moment. I *don't* know everything—nor do I need to. I have discovered that much of life is a mystery. My faith has enlarged.

And come next spring, you will find me still picking strawberries.

Patti Sellers Bubna (Arizona) is Director of Communications at Scottsdale Bible Church. First widowed when her three daughters were very young, she married Paul Bubna seventeen years later. After seven joyous months, he died unexpectedly of a heart attack.

"Learning Not to Walk"

BY LYNNE M. BAAB

After knee surgery, when the doctor told me I couldn't walk for exercise anymore, I had to reframe the way I view life, which is no longer a panorama of unlimited possibilities. I was never physically fit enough to climb Mount Everest, but then I never wanted to climb Mount Everest, so I wasn't bothered by that limitation. This was the first large limitation that had truly changed my life.

Because walking with my husband had been such an integral part of our relationship, I was feeling particularly blue one evening after swimming laps in the pool, so I decided to treat myself to some relaxing minutes in the hot tub. Lowering myself into the water, I hated my life and my body, always longing to be thinner. But as I sat in that hot tub, wishing I were thinner, I looked up, almost as if drawn by God's voice, and saw a woman so overweight that she couldn't wear a swimming suit. She had a roll of stomach fat that drooped down her thighs, and she walked slowly, with discomfort, by the hot tub. I was filled with compassion for her because of what she had to face every day of her life.

I could almost hear God's voice saying to me, "You may be overweight, but it doesn't affect your life the way this woman's weight does hers. Are you going to be grateful for what you have, or are you going to continue to complain about what you don't have?"

I sat in that hot tub feeling grateful for about four seconds. Then I began to feel sorry for myself about my knee. I miss walking so much. I miss the random thoughts that come through my mind when I'm walking alone, thoughts triggered by luxurious gardens and racing clouds. I miss the rambling conversations with my husband, our thoughts moving in various directions because of the rhythm of our feet on the pavement. I was almost in tears, sitting in that hot tub, missing walking.

I got out of the hot tub and wandered morosely into the dressing room. On my way to the shower, I saw a woman entering the dressing room pushing an empty wheelchair. I wondered why the chair was empty.

I took my shower. As I walked to my locker, I passed that woman, now sitting in a secluded dressing area, the wheelchair beside her. She had taken off her clothes and was in the process of removing a prosthetic leg that extended up to the middle of her thigh. Obviously she was going to use the wheelchair to get herself to the pool. I was complaining about the limitations of having a left knee that gets sore easily; the woman in the locker room didn't have a left knee at all.

For the second time that day, I could hear God's voice asking me if I was going to be grateful for what I have or if I was going to continue to focus on what I don't have. As I enter my fifties, I know very clearly that there will be continual losses for the rest of my life. In fact, from my observations of people of various ages, the losses will accelerate. Friends and family members will die, and I will grieve deeply. There will be health issues, both for myself and for the people I love. I will watch both good and bad things happen to my kids, my husband, my family and friends, and I will not be able to control any of these things. I know there will be pain, and I won't like it one little bit.

I hope I can grieve for the losses that I will undoubtedly experience, and at the same time be deeply aware of the many blessings of my life. I hope I can leave behind the naiveté of the first half of life that believes that a continual stream of good things will happen. I want to be deeply honest about the pain of the losses, and I also want to be deeply thankful for the many good things that crowd my life.

I have a loving husband, two kids who are out of the nest exploring the world, a wonderful job with interesting things to do every day, friends and family members whom I love, and a nice house in a great neighborhood. These are huge blessings. There are also so many small blessings that I can overlook so easily. A bite of a delicious salad, the sweet and tart flavors intermingling. The evening sun reflecting off the cedar tree in our yard. A light breeze on a warm day. A touch on my shoulder just when I need it. Being prayed for. The right word from a friend when I need encouragement.

I have been thinking lately about Georgia O'Keeffe's flower paintings. I learned last year that she began to paint those huge flowers when she was living in New York City. She came there after living in the wide-open spaces of the West, and she found it difficult to be surrounded by crowded sidewalks and tall buildings that obscured the sky and the sun. She began to look intentionally at the small, beautiful things in her life, and she discovered the complexity and wonder of the detail in flowers.

She often chose to paint petunias, those ordinary flowers that thrive in so many different conditions. When we look at one of her petunias that fill a large canvas, with all the detail and colors inside the bloom, we don't know where she found that petunia. Maybe it was planted in a window box on a sooty Manhattan window. Maybe it was growing beside a littered sidewalk, or struggling to survive in a small weedy flower bed in Central Park. O'Keeffe chose to ignore the surroundings and notice the flower, focusing intently on its small-scale beauty.

That's what I am learning to do. I hope and pray that my fifties are marked by thankfulness for all of God's beauty and blessings that come to me every day, even if—as happens all too often—these bountiful gifts are intermingled with things I don't like at all. Every day, aspects of my life are as beautiful as a flower, and I want to notice them and give thanks to the Giver of every good and perfect gift (see James 1:17 KJV). I want to age gracefully. I don't want to be one of those people who have nothing but negative things to say. At the same time, I don't want to be falsely cheerful with a pasted-on smile. I want to be honest about the losses and pain that are inevitable in the second half of life. But I also want to be aware of the precious gift of life with all its large and small blessings so that I can age with grace and love.

Lynne M. Baab (Washington) is an associate pastor at Bethany Presbyterian Church in Seattle and the author of several books including *A Renewed Spirituality: Finding Fresh Paths at Midlife, Beating Burnout in Congregations*, and *Personality Type in Congregations*.

"Lost Years"

BY PATRICIA G. GILBERT

Me, the mother of the bride? I'm too young for this! Didn't I just become an empty nester last year? How did this happen? The truth is, it happens to all of us when children grow up and start living their own lives. And even though major milestones often catch me by surprise, the truth is that I am enjoying the happiest and most blessed time in my life.

I am a child of the living God and have been blessed with a godly husband and three beautiful children. My counseling practice involves me in fulfilling ministry, I have good health, and I am having great joy in all I'm doing.

It's hard to believe now that when my daughter, the bride, Jennifer Elizabeth, was only a baby, I succumbed to total darkness and experienced an extended stay in a psychiatric ward. Only God could work such a restoration: "Patricia, daughter, don't be afraid. Trust Me. Trust Me with the treasures of your heart. For as I have promised in My Word, 'I myself will search for my sheep and look after them'" (Ezek. 34:11).

When I was nineteen I married a man fourteen years my senior with a host of emotional problems and addictions. When I became pregnant with Jennifer, I still thought my life looked pretty good. I had received my college degree in early childhood education. My husband was well respected with a good job, and we lived in a comfortable house complete with two cars, a dog, a cat, and a beautiful, healthy baby boy, Paul.

But on the inside, my life was heavily burdened. I was in a marriage that I knew in my spirit was not a good one. At age twenty-four I was also the sole caregiver of my failing mother-in-law (who was suffering from the final stages of lung cancer), on top of being a full-time mother to our active twenty-month-old son. I was trying to carry all this responsibility—but my house was built on sand and not on the solid foundation of the Rock.

This was the family situation into which my sweet daughter was born. Jennifer and I instantly shared a close bond, and the nursing staff of Hartford Hospital respected my request to nurse my new baby immediately after delivery. Such wonderful memories I keep as one keeps one's most valuable possessions, tucked safely in my heart, not to be taken from me.

But by the time Jennifer was ten and a half months old, I was sinking fast. I know now that the Lord was with me the whole time, even though I was totally unable to realize it then. I was simply breaking apart—physically, emotionally, psychologically, and spiritually. I had lost control of my life and felt I was dying, sinking into a total blackness.

One fateful night, the Lord used Jennifer's cries to save my life. Since I couldn't handle my husband's drinking or our deteriorating relationship, I was no longer sleeping in the bedroom. While downstairs in the nearly lightless family room—a room I called the "dungeon"—I realized that something was terribly wrong with me. I had gone to my internist just days before, but somehow he hadn't heard what I was trying to tell him. I was alone, and I knew I was in some kind of terrible trouble.

By 4:00 AM I felt myself slipping into darkness. Sapped of strength, I had given up. In the void, I heard Jennifer crying in her crib, cries that were calling me back to consciousness. I became rational just long enough to know I needed to be in a protected environment, perhaps a hospital where others could help me. My husband, finally realizing I was in crisis, called an ambulance. With nothing physically wrong, I was offered a bed in the psychiatric unit, and I took it.

I know now all this happened only by God's grace. Jennifer always slept through the night—always—but not that particular night. God truly does have a plan for me, just as He says in Jeremiah 29:11: "For I know the plans I have for you, … plans to prosper you and not to harm you, plans to give you hope and a future."

When I entered the hospital, I was in such terrible condition that I needed to be watched twenty-four hours a day. When I was brought to the psychiatric unit, my last conscious thought was of telling the nurse she seemed like an angel. I felt safe at last, safe enough to fall into what I thought was only a peaceful sleep. Instead I slid into darkness for nine full days, of which my only memory is the small snippets of time when I was singing Christmas carols to a very sad woman in the ward.

How wondrous our Lord is, as He reached through the darkness to bring me back to Himself, to Life. He is indeed "the way, the truth and the life" (John 14:6 KJV). Because my body and mind had gone through such trauma and shock, it was four months before I was able to go home to live and take care of my children. With the grace of God, I did just that. During that time, the Lord put a need in my heart to find out more about Him and to trust Him. He also put a hunger in my heart to somehow learn His Word. In His perfect timing, I did that as well.

It was a challenging journey. After my initial healing, all of these things took time, prayer, and trust. Right from the beginning I had to trust the Lord with the very treasures of my heart—Jennifer and her older brother Paul. During my illness, little Jennifer was safely taken into my sister's home. With Auntie Emily and Uncle Joe, Jennifer was surrounded by love. Unfortunately, Paul was left in the care of his father, and to this day I don't know all that happened to him during those months. I still pray diligently for Paul, trusting with all my heart that the Lord is in control of his life. Yet I can't deny that Jennifer had a terrifying experience the night I left home, when she woke up to find no mommy to care for her. For her own internal protection and safety, Jennifer must have put up a wall around herself. Her little world was being turned upside down as she entered her second year of life.

Ultimately, I was back with her, trying to rebuild our home and my life. But she received one more blow when I decided I had to divorce her father, who, at this point, was actually starting to put our children's very lives in danger. How could I ever get a two-year-old, who loved her father, to understand such heavy adult concepts? The wall she had built to keep all the pain and fear from her heart grew thicker and thicker, until not even my love could break through it. She was afraid to trust me, to come to me, to talk with me. She was afraid to share her life with me. I had a daughter, yet somehow I didn't. That wall stayed up for many years, no matter how much I loved her.

As always, the Lord has His plan, not only for me, but for each of us. Even though we can't see all He is doing, we can know that God is in control. We have the blessed assurance that "he who began a good work in [us] will carry it on to completion" (Phil. 1:6). We can most assuredly trust Him with our hopes, our dreams, and, yes, our treasures. I have a decorative plaque on my side table: "Love finds a way." God is not only Life, He is Love—and Love's name is Jesus. Jesus has found a way through the wall of my daughter's heart.

Jesus has also used our shared love of animals, especially horses, to further widen the crack in that now crumbling wall. What fun and laughter Jennifer and I have been having together in recent years. We have even shared the heartbreak and tears of sadness when the tough things came along. We've been creating an abundance of new memories for me to treasure. How thankful I am, as I have watched the Lord heal and restore my daughter and our relationship.

Life keeps getting better and better, fuller and fuller. This is truly the most blessed time in my life as I experience God's promised restoration: "I will restore to you [what] the locust has eaten" (Joel 2:25 ESV) God is so good! My hope is only in Him. My eyes are on Him alone. Not only has He restored my life, He continues daily to restore the treasures of my heart.

Patricia G. Gilbert (Florida) is a counselor and Bible teacher. As a licensed Christian Pastoral Counselor, Patricia counsels individuals and couples in the healing presence, power, and truth of Christ Jesus. She and her husband David have three grown children.

"Transforming Losses"

BY CAROLE LEWIS

When I was younger and heard stories of tragedy and loss in the lives of others, I would think to myself how blessed I was that nothing like that had ever happened to me. One of the biggest lessons I have learned since turning fifty is that if nothing bad has happened to us, it is simply because we haven't lived long enough. As we grow older, we will inevitably experience pain in one area or another.

The first real loss I ever experienced was in 1976 when my father died. At the ripe old age of thirty-four I remember vividly thinking that my dad, who was sixty-seven at the time, had lived a rich, full life. My mom was sixty-three, and her entire life had been consumed with loving my father and her two girls. Not until I experienced the pain of loss myself did I fully understand the enormous loss my mother experienced the day my father died. Mom was a daily, living example to me of how pain either destroys or transforms. I watched my mother, who had never worked a day outside our home, become self-sufficient and take charge of all the challenging areas of life she had never tackled before.

She learned how to pay the bills and balance her checkbook. She was able to sell my dad's car, their bay house, his boat, and eventually the home they had lived in for more than twenty years. As God became her husband, He helped her buy a condo where many friends from our church lived. She made new friends with other women who had been widowed, and they would play cards till midnight almost every night. I believe the sweetest thing I ever heard my mother say was that every morning when she was praying she would say to God, "What wonderful thing do You have planned for me today?" My mom had learned through the pain of loss that even though her life would never be the same, it didn't mean her life was over.

My mother's example has inspired me since October 1997 when my own husband was diagnosed with stage-four prostate cancer. That day is indelibly imprinted in my mind. When we heard the news, I began to cry, and I shed buckets of tears for the next three days. Since I was not the one with cancer, I was even more distressed that I couldn't be strong for my husband. After three long days of crying and praying, I looked at my husband early one morning and said, "I'm so sorry that I can't be strong for you right now." Johnny looked at me and said, "How do you think I would feel if you weren't crying?" We both had a good laugh at that, and as we prayed together for strength the transformation from pain to power began. Today, as I write these words, it has been almost six years since Johnny's diagnosis, and praise God, Johnny is not only alive but doing well. Yes, he still has cancer, but he is thriving and grateful to God for His goodness and mercy.

We have learned so many lessons as we have walked this road together. Knowing that we may not have another day together has helped us appreciate the one we have today. We don't waste time worrying about the small stuff anymore. We take time to enjoy every sunrise and sunset we can view together. God has shown us that life is uncertain at best and that I could die before Johnny, so we need to savor every moment of every day. Why did it take a cancer diagnosis for us to realize that the gift of marriage is precious? I don't know the answer to that question, but I do know that I have learned that every day is a gift and that none of us are guaranteed another one on this earth.

Thanksgiving night, 2001, was a night of pain that is forever etched in my memory. Our precious daughter Shari was hit and killed by an eighteen-year-old girl who chose to drive drunk. Shari was thirty-nine years old and left behind her husband, Jeff, and three daughters: Cara, nineteen; Christen, fifteen; and Amanda, thirteen. Shari and her family had spent the day at our house with the rest of our family and left at 4:00 PM to have dinner with Jeff's family. Before they left, Shari decorated my Christmas tree, as was her tradition each year. My last memory of Shari was of Jeff standing there saying, "Shari, we are going to be late. It's four o'clock, and they are eating at five." Shari was putting the final finishing touches to my nautical Christmas tree and saying, "I'm almost through. It will just be another few minutes." I could write an entire book about the goodness of our God since that sad day. Suffice it to say that God does not take it lightly when His children suffer. God has been there for our family every step of this painful journey, even to the point of giving Cara two Christian friends who also lost a parent during this same time period.

My dear mom died on January 3, 2003, after spending the last three years of her life in my home. She was three months short of her ninetieth birthday. My mom is my hero, and I miss her so much. She left a lasting legacy of love in my life. A legacy that says I have no option but to be transformed by life's pain if I am to be used by God to minister grace to everyone I meet. I am learning that the things that happen to me are really not about me at all. They are about the transforming power of God to take the broken pieces of our lives and make them beautiful once again. I have heard it said, "With age comes wisdom." May those words be said of us all as we grow older.

Carole Lewis (Texas) is the national director of First Place, a Christ-centered health program used in more than 12,000 churches. She is the author of *Choosing to Change, First Place, Today is the First Day, Back on Track,* and *The Mother-Daughter Legacy.* www.FirstPlace.org

Truth Six:

Life Is Full of Surprises

"Controlled Burning"

BY LUCINDA SECREST MCDOWELL

The fire had left its devastation, for everything around us was black and charred. There were no tall grasses left, no underbrush, no wildflowers.

I looked up at Daddy with wide-eyed, ten-year-old amazement. "I can't believe you decided to burn down Brookside."

Brookside was our family's small farm just outside town, a place where we fished, hunted, played, rode horses, and spent campouts at the cabin dubbed by my parents as "The Last Resort."

"Oh, Cindygirl, I didn't burn down Brookside," Daddy replied with a grin. "This is what's called 'controlled burning'—setting carefully guarded fires to clean out the underbrush and make way for new spring growth. Remember, I'm a forester. This is what we foresters do every year."

I wanted to believe Daddy, but the blackened ground didn't look like it would ever see green again. Tentatively I sought to grasp what he had said. "So, it only *looks* like you destroyed Brookside, but what you were really doing is preparing it for new growth?"

"Exactly. Those weeds and tall grasses would have choked back the new plants and flowers this coming spring. So we clear that away, and before you know it, this whole area will be covered in beautiful green grass again," Daddy explained.

For another moment I experienced an internal battle between the *sight I saw* as destroyed land and *the person I trusted* as telling me it was most definitely not the end of all living, growing things at Brookside.

I knew that my daddy loved Brookside—that he enjoyed walking through the trails and boating on the two ponds and driving the jeep from the brooks that bordered each side of the acreage. I also knew that he was a tree planter as well as a forester, that he always replenished the lands that provided wood for his business. Most of all, I knew that he was a person I could believe with all my heart.

But God loves to surprise us. And you know what? By the very next weekend there were tiny shoots of green peeking up all over the farm!

What do you see when you look around your life today? Is there devastation? Have dreams been shattered? Are resources depleted? It's pretty easy to believe that what you see must be the final reality. But you may be wrong. The burned-out brush of your life right now may very well be a carefully "controlled burning" orchestrated by your heavenly Father to provide ideal conditions for new growth. Maybe something in your life has to go so that God could replace it with something even better.

Remember, life is full of surprises!

Lucinda Secrest McDowell, M.T.S. (Connecticut) presents "Encouraging Words that Transform" through her international conference speaking and writing. A graduate of Gordon-Conwell Seminary, she is the author of five books including *Quilts from Heaven, Women's Spiritual Passages,* and *Amazed by Grace.* www.EncouragingWords.net

"I Never Dreamed It Would Be This Way"

BY LINDA RILEY

Experiencing life as a teenager in the youth-obsessed sixties warped my view of growing older—we hippies dreaded turning twenty-five! I left home at sixteen, moved to San Francisco, dropped out, dropped acid, wore flowers in my hair, and marched in protest marches. Eventually, I had no connection whatsoever with anyone older than twenty-something. That, and the diatribes in the "Free Press," and the rock and roll mantra emphasizing the ignorance of adults, and the political activism of the day, all contributed to my indoctrination. To me, twenty-five-year-olds were hopelessly out of touch, and there was no life after thirty. No life worth living, anyway.

While I really haven't spent much time worrying about how "old" looks on the outside, I have had to battle with what "old" might feel like on the inside. When fears of aging overtake me, what worries me is the possibility of suffering from a brittle brain, filled with dated data. I fret about fossilized feelings, antiquated attitudes, rigid reasoning. Or, worse yet, a hardening of the heart, a withering of the spirit.

When I was still in my teen years, a young man introduced me to Jesus Christ, and my views on life began to change, but not my views on growing older. Even the church culture of the day was youth-obsessed. I unknowingly joined what became known as the Jesus Movement, widely known as a youth revival. Our little church was packed with hippies, bikers, high school kids, all kinds of young people getting saved, delivered from crime, drugs, alcohol, and giving their testimonies. Reporters came from all over the world to report on our church's part in the Jesus Movement.

We prayed by the hour, went street witnessing each night, and won people to the Lord left and right. Life was extremely exciting, when I was fellowshipping with "my generation," that is. Once in a while, we would have elderly guest speakers and ministers at church, singing ancient hymns off pitch or giving historic testimonies about being delivered from their former sinful "flapper" or "bootlegger" lifestyles many long years ago. I would look at my friends blankly and think, *Oh boy, isn't that exciting? About as exciting as a lecture in a museum.*

We were frequently exhorted that "It is good for a man to bear the yoke in his youth" (Lam. 3:27 NKJV). We wanted to pack in all the ministry we could before we "fossilized." We fretted that getting married and having children would hinder our work for the Lord—so many tracts, so little time. Growing older seemed to be synonymous with growing lukewarm in the faith. On my twenty-first birthday I grieved for my lost youth.

Like all revival movements, the Jesus Movement came from God, refused to be forever sustained by man, and gradually receded into history. My Christian life normalized, but my idolization of youth remained. My thirtieth birthday was more like a wake than a party. I was relieved when the actual event was over.

But I was in for a gradual surprise. Life continued on, and it was good. The rhetoric was not true. The whole culture was perpetuating a lie. There *was* life after thirty—meaningful life, fruitful life, rewarding life, spiritual life, life in abundance, all after thirty. Rather than just shriveling up and disappearing, I went on to truly enjoy my thirties. Active in nonprofit work, growing closer in my marriage, beginning to raise a family, life was full and held out many promises of fulfilling days to come. If I felt this good in my thirties, if life was still this interesting, this inviting, then perhaps every decade could bring the sweet surprises that come into a life well lived.

A few years into my thirties, I was in Seattle for a Christian organization's board meeting. I drove our director to a radio interview that permanently changed my view of growing older in the Lord. When the program hostess greeted us, I noticed many remarkable things about her. She was beautifully groomed, but more striking was her personal demeanor: warm, gracious, confident, reassuring. Her face shone with obvious enjoyment of her work and ministry. Her life seemed an everyday adventure, and everyone around her was invited to join in. I also noticed that she had to be about sixty-something.

Filled with admiration, I began to think, *This is the future of the godly woman: an adventure with God at every age and stage of life.* I began to look more closely at the lives of other older Christian women I knew, those who were graciously living a meaningful, purposeful, divinely ordered life all of their days. Instead of depression and grief over growing older, a new expectation filled my heart. An expectation that life can always be challenging, interesting, exciting, and fulfilling.

By forty, I was on my way to honoring my hard-won maturity and all the experience, perspective, and wisdom that the mature acquire. Still, as a final homage to youth I threw myself an unusual party for my fortieth birthday. Rather than the black "over-the-hill" theme, I decided to take my inner child out for the day. I threw a "retro-party," a replica of the childhood parties of the fifties and early sixties that my mother threw for me.

Guests arrived to the tunes of Shirley Temple and went to a craft table to design their own party hats, with a contest for the best. We ate peanut butter and jelly canapés, celery and cheese "pirate boats," Kool-Aid frappés, or Bosco Chocolate Milk and cupcakes with gumdrop teddy bears on top. We played musical chairs and pin the tail on the donkey. We made a big circle and danced the Hokey Pokey. I even hired a local actress "mom" to dress like Donna Reed with heels, housedress, apron, pearls, and beehive hairdo, and to coerce all the more reasonable adults in the crowd to actually dance the Hokey Pokey. My hired mom ran the whole party as my inner child enjoyed her big fling.

I have needed a sense of humor to navigate the many startling twists and turns on the road of life. I never thought I would marry a minister, and no one who knew me in my growing-up years thought so either. I never thought a woman like me, not able to bear children, would end up with eight, dropped onto the doorstep of my heart, a few at a time. I never thought I would have cancer, or that I would survive it if I did. I never thought my knee-knocking first public speech would lead to a speaking career that I would grow to enjoy.

I never thought I would love my thirties and my forties. But I did. And I have made up my mind to enjoy the rest of the gift of life as well. I don't exactly know how to prepare for the future, except to hold Jesus' hand on the walk through today. Jesus is enough. And one nice thing about getting older is that we have had to learn that truth so many times that we know it well by now.

Jesus is enough. Life is not found in work, or in family, or in the mirror. Life is found in Christ. And Christ is the same, yesterday, today, and even tomorrow (see Heb. 13:8). Even on the tomorrow when I turn fifty, even on the tomorrow when my invitation to join the AARP comes in the mail, even on the tomorrow when the kid at the movie ticket counter asks me for the very first time if I would like to take advantage of the senior discount. Even on those tomorrows. And even on the tomorrow when all the tomorrows merge into eternity, and there is no age at all.

Linda Riley (California) is a pastor's wife, mother of eight, speaker, and author of *The Call to Love*. She is also the founder of Called Together Ministries, a resource and support organization for clergy families, and was a columnist for *Leadership Journal*. www.learntolove.org.

"Seeds of Summer"

BY MARTA D. BENNETT

My last few years have seemed a time of spring blossoms mellowing into summer fruit. Childhood up through the teen years was like the winter sojourn, a time of testing and of preparation. Spring was the blossoming forth into my own person, purposefully exploring potentials and somehow making a contribution in work and ministry through professional life. Now it is summer; the blossoms have developed into fruit, and the fruit is maturing. Some of this fruit has taken surprising forms and colors. Some of what was so important before has become so neglected that it has fallen away; some has been bruised, shaken, or lopped off. Parts of me have been left behind and remain as mere memories, but a certain portion has flourished and is growing ripe and sweet, with new sprouts pushing through.

So what has the summer season of my life held so far? As I have heard others so aptly say about this stage of life, I have felt a shift from seeking growth and success to seeking significance, moving from a focus on *accomplishment* to a focus on *purpose*. I am at a place where no one really knows—or cares—who or what I was before. They only know me now, in this context. This brings both freedom and a great challenge. Even if I wanted to live on past glories, no one here is particularly interested, or even would know what I was talking about. They don't care about all the frenetic activities I was involved in earlier in life, which led me to this place.

Living in Kenya, in the midst of a culture in which relationships are far more valued than tasks, I have been forced to slow down, to be willing to be interrupted at any moment for any amount of time. Africa has taught me to be a generous hostess, something which my beautiful and gracious mother tried to teach me for years, but for which I was a slow and miserable student in my growing-up years.

My vocation as a pastor and teacher of adults has not changed; it is still the same. The change, however, is that now what matters is my purpose more than my position, giving more than collecting, focusing on one thing instead of the many things, being and deepening instead of becoming, getting, and doing. Significance in the light of eternity is more important than contemporary success. When I was younger, I had once declared that if I was to burn out, I wanted to burn out for Jesus, not missing any opportunity to serve Him. But now I ask, "What is effective, what will make a difference for Jesus' sake? What will really matter when I look back on my life from God's perspective, when my age is old and ripe?" Not, "Is this important?" but, "Is this essential?"—which is the essence of what is truly important.

One unanticipated and complete surprise has been the adoption of two Kenyan children. At the end of November 1997, out of the blue I began being plagued by the overwhelming cases of abandoned children and infants in Nairobi. This was not new news, but somehow the reality began pounding on my conscience, with the sensation that perhaps I should adopt one, a feeling that I could not shake. I kept trying to brush the idea out of my mind, suspecting that it would not even be an option, seeing that I was in my forties, single, non-Kenyan, and white. But I couldn't shake it, so after a month of intense inner struggle, I finally went to visit a home for abandoned and HIV-infected infants to inquire about options and even procedures. Half of my heart said that perhaps this visit would put to rest the plaguing tugs; the other half wondered what God was up to. By the end of that visit, I had met Justin, just one month old. He was the last child I met that day, just as I was leaving; he was out on the porch in a stroller because he was always crying too much. There was something about his bright eyes, his wild shock of black baby hair, and his strong legs that insisted on pushing him up, that captured me. Two weeks later he came home with me, just six weeks old.

During the two weeks between meeting Justin and his coming home, I had fervently prayed for God's wisdom and direction, and urgently sought the counsel of several who know me well. As I was pondering the option, I had prayed, "Lord, this is crazy, but if this is of You, then may it not be just one, but eventually two." I felt strongly that, when possible, it is better for a child to grow up with a sibling, not as an only child. Not quite two years later when Justin was twenty-two months old, Imani (Swahili for "Faith") joined our family. She had been born several months premature, and had been abandoned by her birth mother in the public hospital. Her medical chart merely read: "Premature; jaundice, anemia, pneumonia; mother absconded." Born at just over two pounds, by the age of two and a half months when she was brought to the children's home, she had made it to four pounds. I met her the next day. In October 1999, Sara Imani Njeri Bennett joined our small family, and even now, people often observe that the two children look so much alike. When I am asked, "Are they actually brother and sister?" I reply, "Yes, they are now!"

Having two children when I had been making peace with being single, and therefore had resigned myself to not having children of my own, God has blessed me beyond my prayers. I chuckle sometimes when I think of the funny twists in life. While the children of my friends back in the States are scouring the Internet and university catalogues for where to apply for college or graduate school, I am looking into preschool options for mine. My own identity has changed drastically, and instead of being known as the "Rev. Dr.," a number of those with whom I interact daily know me only as "Mama Justin"(mother of Justin). I find this a great honor, and somehow satisfying. Again, relationships are reinforced, not accomplishments. Instead of the Western declaration of "I think, therefore I am," I have become more at home with the African "I am because we are, and because we are, therefore I am."

I have spent days on end at the gate of a refugee camp, urging the release of some of our African international students who were unjustly arrested, and I have eaten the sweetest pineapple, roasted maize, and Zanzibar charbroiled fish or roasted goat, sitting on the doorsteps of students' thatched rural homes. How could I think of forfeiting the sight of the red sun setting over the Ngong Hills, or of watching the graceful stride of a giraffe strolling across the road on my way out to the university? I have witnessed carjackings, and U.S. embassy bombings, but God continues to show His faithfulness in small and big ways day by day. It is a privilege to live and work with people in this part of the world so different from my own upbringing.

I have changed, and hopefully deepened. Though I was city born and bred, my heart now skips a beat with concern when I hear someone dejectedly mention that two more cows have died in the drought. I am delighted when a worker presents our urban household with a live chicken, which we will keep in the downstairs bathroom at night until the chicken becomes dinner later in the week. (But I must confess, I still ask our African neighbors to do "the honors," to kill and pluck the victim. I am too much of an American city girl to manage preparing any chicken that doesn't come in plastic wrap.) My ear has become attuned to Swahili, French, and English with a variety of accents, and my own speech has become peppered with words and phrases that I have to consciously set aside when I visit the States on furlough. My children dance and clap at the sound of worship, and school means smartly pressed uniforms and well-penciled exercise books.

My experience has been ripening under the African sun, as I near the end of my seventh year living in East Africa. I told my graduate students the other day that instead of my litany of activities and involvements that defined my identity before, I now have just two pillars on which I hang my identity.

First, my foundation is Christ. I find that my faith has grown simpler, not more complex. As I daily witness the suffering and challenges of so many all around me, my faith has come to be summed up in two brief phrases: "Life is hard; God is good." When one forgets either half, one gets in trouble.

Second, my passion is leadership development. I am a teacher deep down, a trainer, equipper, with a side-gift of compassion. I love seeing the unlikely ones rise up and make a difference. I thrive on seeing people come to believe in what God has for them, and to watch them discover that God fully intends to use them too—to influence others to make a difference for His kingdom. I always have. I probe for ways to surprise them into learning or accomplishing something, and I savor the delight that follows for all involved. Now, I more purposefully pursue the leadership development of others, especially of my students and my children. In the summer of my life, perhaps it is more that I am the gardener—they will be the fruit that will carry seeds to plant, nurture, and harvest in future seasons.

Marta D. Bennett (Kenya), a Seattle native, is an ordained Presbyterian pastor. After twelve years at Seattle Pacific University, she joined Daystar University in Nairobi. Currently the Chair of Postgraduate Studies, she is the mother of two Kenyan children. mbennett@maf.or.ke

"A River Runs Down It"

BY CHARLENE ANN BAUMBICH

For Christmas last year, I received a wonderful and very useful gift: a fanny pack (to help balance my built-in fanny pack) that also holds a drink bottle. Since I am undoubtedly Queen of the Perpetual Drink Sippers, it was, indeed, a handy item.

Before George and I left on our annual trek to the local county fair, I filled 'er up and strapped 'er on. After walking around for about an hour and finishing a second tank full, so to speak, it was time to hit the john. Right away!

Since it was a very hot, sticky day, and since a strapped-on fanny pack makes loosening clothing so much more difficult, I unsnapped it from around my waist and hung it around my neck so I could negotiate the necessities without impairment. In the nick of time, I was free to do my duty. Whew! But by mid-stream, a horrible sensation struck me. Rather it started running down the inside of my left leg after having passed through the crotch of my downed shorts. In the heat and desperateness of disencumbering myself from the tacky clothes, I must not have gotten something pulled down right. To make it worse, it was beyond my capabilities to shut off the tap, so to speak. I was stunned, humiliated, and wet.

Then the light finally dawned. I hadn't secured the pop-up top on the drink bottle, and since I was bent over and it dangled from my neck, this allowed the water to pour right into my pants. Although my shorts were a wet mess, I was relieved to find out that the situation wasn't what I first believed it to be.

But relief was brief because suddenly I saw them—the dancing feet of the lady in the stall next to me. The stream of water that had run down my leg had quickly flowed in her direction. Of course she didn't know the stream originated from my water bottle, so I quickly hollered, "It's not what you think. It's my water bottle."

My reassurance did nothing to stop those dancing feet that were trying to hover, one at a dancing time, above the floor and out of the stream.

I exited the stall before her and dutifully waited to show her exactly what had happened. I had become nearly hysterical with laughter by this point, not only for the absurdity of the episode, but also at the vision of my shorts which were entirely soaked right where they shouldn't be.

When the lady exited her stall, through my peels of laughter I tried to give her a quick demo as to what had happened. She didn't laugh, she didn't smile, she didn't wash her hands. She simply left me standing alone wearing wet pants, babbling and laughing. The next lady who entered the bathroom took a swift up-and-down look at me and didn't laugh either.

Dear Lord, thanks for helping me to laugh at myself. Especially when I'm the only one who thinks I'm funny. Okay, so the joke's on me, but at least I get it!

Charlene Ann Baumbich (Illinois) hasn't stopped laughing at herself yet. The author of the *Dearest Dorothy* series, Charlene now joyfully "resides" in Partonville, where oldsters are young, trees have names, and cars don't fly. Stop by www.WelcomeToPartonville.com

"Have I Got What It Takes to Start Over?"

BY VIRELLE KIDDER

You're kidding, right?" I asked, looking my husband straight in the eye.

"Warm weather is calling my name," Steve repeated his theme song with a boyish smile. "Why not move? Maybe live on a sailboat? We're still young enough to change lifestyles. It will be fun."

Granted, early retirement was a fleeting daydream we both entertained, and browsing through Florida house plans and boating magazines had become our favorite mental retreat on these dreary late-winter days in the northeast. Who wouldn't trade sleet and freezing rain for white sand and warm trade winds? But move almost thirty years of family memories? Impossible. Reinventing my life after all these years seemed out of the question.

I hadn't counted on God's whispers penetrating my thoughts: "I've helped others adjust to a new life. Why not you?"

Softening slightly, I turned to Steve. "I'll think about it." To my husband, that meant yes! Now I needed expert help in attitude adjustment.

Instantly names and faces came to mind, women who had mustered the wherewithal to start life over again and make it work. I guessed what they would say: "Yes, change hurts, but it also liberates and reacquaints us with life. Don't be so afraid." Pushing aside my fantasies and fears, I decided to listen to friends who had handled life's curve balls well. I turned to my dear friend, Judie, and her mom, Ruth.

After twenty-three years of relishing her life as a homemaker with three kids, Judie reentered the work force abruptly when her husband's mid-life job change turned into a nightmare. Within three years her company relocated, offering her a promotion if she would move out of state. It was the only door that opened. In what seemed like minutes, their beautiful country home was sold, and they were gone. Those of us on the quiet side of the door missed them daily.

Judie recalled the sense of loss: "The biggest challenge was leaving behind all our history, leaving a place where all those years I was at home, being involved at school and at church, enjoying all those wonderful relationships. All of a sudden I didn't have any of it anymore."

That's the part that scares me most about change. How had she coped? "You do the next thing," she reflected softly. "It's not a down time, it's just a change. It's like anything else. The Lord will give you what you need to do whatever He has called you to do."

Judie's quiet courage doesn't surprise me. She has spent a lifetime watching her mom's example. Soon after their move, Ruth responded to their invitation to live closer by selling her family home of forty-four years, moving more than a thousand miles east, and building a new one. Excitedly, she described every room in detail. I asked her how she had made it look so easy, even fun.

"It's not hard when God leads you," Ruth giggled. Even over the phone, I could picture her sitting with legs crossed, leaning forward with enthusiasm, her face tilted upward in a smile. Well into her eighties, this mentoring mom never failed to encourage me, or prod me away from an easy faith.

"After the movers left," she continued, "I went through the house and said good-bye in every room, locked up, and took the keys to the folks who had bought it. Then, I took a hot bath and went to bed. I slept like a baby."

Ruth is no stranger to starting life over. When her husband collapsed suddenly in their home and died of a massive coronary in the arms of their two teen-aged sons, and again several years later when the younger of those sons was killed instantly in a motorcycle accident, Ruth learned to lean hard on God. "Don't neglect your relationship with God," she cautioned. "Walk with Him every day consciously. We may get a few detours, but His plan will work in our lives no matter what it is. We can trust Him. That has been the guiding force in my life."

Listening to the graduate-level changes my friends have survived made our possible move to a sunny climate look like nursery school. I knew God's fingerprints had covered every previous change in our lives. Why stop trusting now? Learning to lean harder on Him through the uncertainties of change will be good for me, even if I am over fifty and a little scared. It's another way He is growing me up.

Now what was the temperature in Miami today?

Virelle Kidder (New York) is an author and conference speaker who loves encouraging women on their spiritual journeys. Her latest book, *Donkeys Still Talk,* is her personal account of meeting God many times when she was neither looking nor listening for Him. www.VirelleKidder.com

"Baby, You Ain't Seen Nothin' Yet!"

BY SUSAN DUKE

The *word* rolled off my tongue like a slothful tumbleweed. Reluctantly, it inched its way across the Texas flatlands, void of the wind's empowering assistance. When it finally reached its destination—somewhere along the dusty roadside of my brain—this strangely unfamiliar word didn't sound right, feel right, or fit my alleged youthful profile. But the *word*, however hard to utter, was formidable—and true.

It didn't matter that in a few short hours I would be attending a huge birthday party with a surprise theme, given in my honor by precious, caring, fun-loving friends. It didn't matter that my husband woke me up whispering that he loves me more today than yesterday. It didn't even matter that a woman I had met a few days before said she could have sworn I was in my late thirties. Nothing—not even the talk show I had seen featuring gorgeous same-age-or-older glamour queens declaring their current age as the most exciting of their lives—made me feel any better.

No, on that particular June morning, as I rolled over in bed, nothing altered the fact that sometime during the night Father Time had paid me a visit and turned the hands on my baby-boomer clock to the big fifty. Words like "middle age" and "AARP" (who, by the way, wasted no time in sending me their senior citizens information packet) raced audaciously across my mind.

It wasn't vanity or fear that jarred me out of a peaceful sleep into shocking reality that morning. I remembered feeling "old" on my thirtieth birthday, and "numb" at forty.

But fifty! Turning fifty is a rite of passage that calls for some real reflection and serious evaluation—not to mention some unambiguous attitude adjustments. The plain truth is ... I wasn't handling this birthday very well. I began asking myself questions like, "Why did I ever hint to my husband that I'd love having a party on *this* birthday? This is the birthday I should tiptoe into without even the slightest whisper to anyone." After all, I didn't think of myself as middle aged, and I certainly didn't want anyone else to either. But now the secret was out.

Despite my feelings and fragile emotions that sunny June morning, I decided to get up, put on the birthday-girl face, and have coffee with my husband and a dear friend, LeAnn, who had flown all the way from Florida the night before especially for my birthday. When she showed up on my doorstep at midnight, ready to show her love and share in the blessed event, I was not only surprised but overjoyed that anyone would sacrificially extend such a precious gesture of friendship to me.

I had no reason to grumble or complain. *I should be ashamed of myself for wishing I could cancel all thoughts, observances, or announcements of my birthday. Having such caring friends is a rare and valuable treasure in this life.* So, I gave myself a good old-fashioned "talkin' to" and determined in my heart that *this* would be the best birthday I had ever had—and that I would choose to believe I wasn't getting older but wiser, more free and fun loving with every year to follow.

"Tell me what to wear," I pleaded with my husband, Harvey,

knowing that he knew all about the theme and the surprise that had been planned.

"Just dress casual. Jeans will be fine," he said.

"Well, where's the party going to be held?" I probed, hoping to get a few clues.

"Don't worry about where it is; you'll love it."

Around 4:00 PM, Harvey, LeAnn, and I piled into the car and drove to a church gymnasium in a nearby town. I could hear live music coming from inside the building as we walked up the sidewalk. When we finally stepped inside the door, I gasped at what I saw. The entire gym had been decorated to the hilt in fifties' memorabilia. The huge hand-painted backdrops of soda fountain motifs, old 45 records and LPs, and jitterbug dancers created an atmosphere that made me feel like I was stepping back in time. As I walked across the floor, the band, dressed in leather jackets and white T-shirts and sporting slicked-back hair, played and belted out the old song, "Suzie Q." Everyone was dressed fifties' style. Ponytails, rolled-up blue jeans, and white bobby socks were the attire of the day. The friends who had worked for six months to pull this off were wearing an assortment of pink, red, blue, and black poodle skirts, and black and white saddle oxfords. They ushered me into a dressing room where they presented me with my very own blue poodle skirt to change into; and later in the evening, they combined their singing talents and made their sensational debut as Betty and the Be-bopettes.

Members of my family from out of town, and friends I had not seen in a very long time were there. The spirited, nostalgic music, the sound of carefree laughter, and the joyful expressions on every face proved that everyone in the room was having a wonderful time. But that wasn't all. When I spied the long tables of food that Marla had prepared, I realized she had cooked every type of dish imaginable that she thought I liked—and every dessert she had ever heard me mention that I loved. For more than a month several members of her family had helped her prepare and freeze enough food to feed a small army of guests—all in my honor.

I'm not sure if I cried more—or laughed more. In between dancing, of course. Yes, I said dancing. Something the majority of the people in the room hadn't done in years. But when special dance numbers like "The Stroll" or "The Twist" were played, everyone forgot their age and danced down memory lane in their sock feet—just as they had done at high school sock hops.

If all that wasn't enough, at one point during the evening, I was declared the party queen and donned with a feather boa and crown. I sat, tears streaming down my cheeks, as Marla and Brenda, their mom Betty, and other family members sang me a medley of songs they had selected for the occasion. The Be-bopettes were so fabulous, I told them they could make a small fortune singing at other events. However, I was surprised when Marla responded, "Baby, you ain't seen nothin' yet!"

Little did I know, the highlight of the party was about to begin. Appearing from behind the curtains on the makeshift stage was none other than Elvis himself. Yep. Elvis. White-satin-caped, rhinestone-stud-suited, wide-rim-gold-sunglass-wearing, black-haired Elvis—singing, "I just wanna be your teddy bear" while handing me a huge stuffed white teddy bear. Elvis (aka Royce, who is Marla's husband) commanded the stage with his larger-than-life, authentic-sounding Elvis impersonation. Knowing that he had never worn an Elvis suit in his life made it all the more special. But to hear a King of Rock and Roll impersonation better than any I had ever heard before was mind-boggling. After an entire concert of Elvis songs, ending with the famous gospel favorites, Elvis threw scarves imprinted with "Love Me Tender" to the screaming fans who had swarmed around the stage.

To say I was overwhelmed would be an understatement. To say I had fun would be like trying to mildly describe the most incredible birthday anyone could ever dream of having. There was nothing mild about my party. There was nothing left undone. Nothing left unsaid or unexpressed. It literally took months for these precious friends to prepare the perfect birthday jubilee for me. They said they hoped and prayed it would be the best birthday of my life. It was. They wanted me to feel special. I did. But the real gift was seeing and experiencing love personified, realizing that even though I thought we had shared the deepest depths of friendship, these friends had invited me to an even deeper place within my heart that I didn't know existed. It's a place where time stands still, and sweet memories never end. It's a place where we are ageless, joyful, innocent, and free. And it's a place where we can believe in new dreams, regardless of birthdays, gray hair, or AARP mail.

Even now, I am moved to tears by the memories of that special night. When the party was over, I arrived back home with my car overflowing with wonderful gifts, cards, a cake decorated with a blonde-haired, purple-caped party queen, and enough joy in my heart to make me forget the blisters on my aching feet. After all, I had found out—I can still dance! And I felt pretty silly and guilty for all of the foreboding, sobering thoughts about turning fifty that I had awakened with that morning. I had found out that age really is irrelevant in the bigger picture of life. One more year hadn't diminished my love for laughter, the enjoyment of friends, the blessing of family, or the blissfully tender empowerment of knowing I am loved.

I will always remember this as the year I learned the best lesson of my life: that birthdays are a gift—and meant to be enjoyed. And with each passing year, I intend to celebrate by saying, "Baby, you ain't seen nothin' yet!"

Susan Duke (Texas) is a wife, mother, popular motivational speaker, and best-selling author/co-author of fourteen books, including *Earth Angels* and *Wolfie's Dream* (from the Schnauzer Chronicles Series). www.SuzieDuke.com

"Grit and Glory"

BY LOUISE TUCKER JONES

It was a minute before midnight. "Quick! Ask me how old I am," I said to my husband, Carl.

"How old are you?"

"Forty-nine!" I said triumphantly. I knew it was the last time I could truthfully make that statement. The next minute, I was fifty in all its "grit and glory." And there had been plenty of both in my life.

The "glory" part was easy. I had a husband and children who loved me, wonderful parents and siblings, a vibrant church, and many friends. Life was going well. My oldest son, Aaron, was a newlywed and teaching school just two hours away. My youngest son, Jay, with Down's syndrome and progressive heart disease, was doing better than doctors ever expected. My writing career was beginning to take off, and my health was good.

The "grit" was the tough stuff. The hard times I had been through. My middle son, Travis, died before we ever got to celebrate a Christmas or birthday with him. My adopted daughter had been a prodigal most of her life, and when she left the last time she took our only grandchild with her. Paula had given birth to two daughters. I was at the hospital when her first child was born prematurely, then at the baby's graveside three months later. Within eighteen months, Paula placed her second daughter in my arms. Monica looked so much like her mother that I felt God had gifted me with the years I missed with Paula, having adopted her at nearly four years of age. Now, they were both gone.

And just four years earlier, I went through a full year of devastating clinical depression after my youngest son nearly died in my arms. These fifty years had not been easy. Not what I dreamed about as a child or even planned as a young woman.

I was going to be a missionary and go to some foreign land. I had planned that since I was nine years old in Vacation Bible School. I even dedicated myself to missions in front of my church when I was sixteen years old. Where had I gone wrong? Why didn't I fulfill my calling? Was it for lack of love? Lack of commitment? Was God disappointed that I wasn't on a foreign shore winning souls for Jesus?

The questions often haunted me, but through the years I finally came to realize that my whole life had actually been a mission field. It wasn't the one I planned, and it certainly wasn't an easy one. My husband and I were married only eight hours before he was shipped overseas. We didn't see each other again for nearly a year and a half. I thought God had forgotten me. But during that time I had the opportunity to know and love Carl's mother, one of the godliest women I have ever known. She died during that year and half, and I would have missed that relationship and the wisdom God taught me through her had I been with my husband, her only child.

When my son Jay was born with Down's syndrome and developed severe progressive heart disease, I asked God why. It wasn't fair. This wasn't what I signed up for. I wanted to be a mother more than anything in my life, yet already I had watched one son die. Now the doctors told me I would lose this child. But through the years, Jay survived and celebrated every ounce of life and showed me a joy I had never known. Today I reach out to hundreds of families with special needs through my writing and speaking. It is definitely a mission field.

The despair I felt in clinical depression cannot be summed up in words. It was like the very breath of hope was drawn from my heart and soul, but when God eventually rolled back the darkness, His radiance shone through me. The silver had been refined. The dross skimmed away in a painful process.

I looked at life in a different way. The way the earth appears after a spring rain. The grass and trees are greener. The yellow, red, pink, coral, and purple blossoms of flowers make such a vibrant contrast to the gray, overcast skies that it looks like an artist's palette.

That's my life, I think to myself. After all the storms and the hard times, the rainbows and silver linings come shining through. They heighten my senses and make me fall to my knees. I know I am in the presence of Deity, aware of my finiteness and God's sovereignty.

Today, those questions from my younger days no longer haunt me: "Did I miss God's will? Did I miss God's best for me?" The answer is an emphatic, "No!" I now understand that God wasn't waiting for me to do the right thing, be the right person, go to the right place. He was doing the right thing with the decisions I made—both good and bad. He took them all and made blessings, joys, adventures, and even mission fields out of them. He put passions in my heart for the gifts He placed in my hands, and He watched over my life, even when I tried to take control.

I know I still have a lot to learn, but I have also learned a lot. One of the greatest of these being that God holds the key to my life. When I am tired, discouraged, sick, afraid, or lonely, God is there. When my heart is weary, and I don't know how to pray, God is there. When everything in my world crumbles and falls, God is there. He is faithful. He always has the answer, even when I don't know the question. That's what I call sovereign love.

Louise Tucker Jones (Oklahoma) is an inspirational speaker and award-winning author of *Dance from the Heart* and co-author of *Extraordinary Kids*. Her work is featured in magazines such as *Guideposts* and *Focus on the Family* as well as a dozen compilation books. LouiseTJ@cox.net

"The Day the Piano Moved Out"

BY CYNTHIA FANTASIA

"Fluttering Leaves" gave me a fluttering stomach. Bach's "Prelude in C" was my prelude to sweaty palms. And the scales ... well, let's not even go there. We were a musical family: my mother and father loved music, my sister played beautifully, but when I sat down at that piano I connected the right notes with the right keys but just couldn't get the right sound. Dutifully though, I practiced, went to recitals, and believed that one day I would "get it."

The years passed, and mercifully I was sent off to college where sorority life, sporting events, and studying filled my heart and my life. My days were rich with friends and exciting activity, yet deep inside I did not feel complete. Every once in a while, that little voice would nag at my spirit, "If only you were able to play, if only you were musical, then you would really be a complete person." And I listened!

For years I lived in the "shadowlands": a wonderful marriage, three great children, a teaching position in a prestigious school system, and a piano in our living room. I "had it all," but at the same time I kept missing something. Our children took piano lessons each week, each day they practiced, and they even played "Fluttering Leaves" and Bach's "Prelude in C" better than I ever did. There was that nagging voice again, "See, if you had practiced more, maybe you could play with them, maybe you would have been a better mother." And I listened!

Over time, sports, schoolwork, and the busy social life of teenagers began to encroach on piano lessons and practice time: "Mom, I just can't get to my lesson today. I have too much homework." "Mom, I have youth group retreat this weekend. How can I go to my piano recital?" "Mom, I just don't have any more time in my life. Do I have to continue to take piano lessons?" And I listened! They seemed to present reasonable arguments: they had taken lessons for many years, they could play the piano for pleasure, what would be the harm in quitting? Was I a failure as a mother? Was I denying them the joy of pressing beyond my own musical accomplishments (small as they were)? And what would we do with the piano in the living room?

Teaching gave way to a call to ministry, and I reveled in how God had given me the deep desire of my heart, to serve Him and pastor the women in our church. At about the same time, Jimmy and Sally came into our lives. He was our kids' youth pastor, and she became a dear friend. How we loved to spend time with them. They became part of our extended family, and we celebrated our friendship. We shared with one another from the deepest places in our hearts: we laughed, cried, and prayed together. Until one day ...

"South Carolina? What do you mean? When are you leaving?" Soon, we were helping them to pack, reminiscing about our days together, and bittersweetly planning our good-byes. "As soon as we get settled in South Carolina, we hope to purchase a piano. Sally loves to play, and we hope our kids will play too. We would love to find a piano just like yours, one that would fit nicely in a parsonage." Was this music to my ears? Every house had to have a piano! I made an immediate decision.

It was a bright, beautiful New England fall day. The leaves were ablaze with color all over our front lawn, and the sun cast a bronze glow through our living room window. There it stood, polished and ready, the seat filled with books and sheet music. Time seemed to stand still. I was alone in the house, alone with my thoughts and my memories. The truck pulled into the driveway. The driver got out, walked to our front door, and the doorbell jangled me back to reality. He smiled, carried the bench out, and returned with the dolly to wheel our piano out the door and into the truck. In an instant it was over. The truck pulled away. I closed the door and looked at that wall—empty and barren after all these years. The house was quiet. All I could hear was the scuff of my shoes on the floor as I walked over to the sofa to sit—in a room without a piano.

In the quietness and stillness of that moment, I wept. This was new, this was strange, this was another world. But life went on, and I learned that life could be full, rich, and complete, even without a piano in the house. That Christmas, the video arrived from Jimmy and Sally. We laughed and we cried as we enjoyed their Christmas gift to us: a piano concert from their living room.

At that moment I came to realize that God had given me music to enjoy from an entirely different source: Him. There was a song in my heart that was just waiting to be sung. That song had a melody unlike any other, and I continue to learn more notes every day. The musical instrument that God gave me to "play" was an open heart, one open to His plan and willing to trust Him with that great unknown. He has given me musical notes in the shape of the spoken word as I teach our weekly Bible study and speak at women's events. He has given me "sheet music" tucked in the pages of Scripture as I dig deep into His Truth. And He has given me the opportunity to practice as I pursue doctoral studies, even as an "old lady."

Zephaniah 3:17 says, "He will take great delight in you, he will quiet you with his love, he will rejoice over you with singing." It takes a while to really hear His music. It took me close to fifty years to hear the song He wrote just for me. If you listen, if you open your hands and your heart, I know you will hear your song. Listen!

Cynthia Fantasia (Massachusetts) is pastor of Women's Ministries at Grace Chapel near Boston, a ministry that draws a thousand women weekly. A popular retreat speaker, Cynthia has written numerous Bible studies. She is married and the mother of three adult children. rcfantasia@earthlink.net

"Shimmer, Glimmer, Sparkle, Joy!"

BY DOLLEY CARLSON

> Do everything ... in which you shine like stars in the universe.
>
> Philippians 2:14–15

Life is full of surprises. Little did I know when making an appointment at a new hair salon that God was sending a joyous new life lesson my way. The hairdresser, "Shanaz from Persia," was delightful and full of enthusiasm.

"You are going to wedding, you should sparkle."

After she put what I thought were the finishing touches on my "do," and before I knew what was happening, she popped gold glitter on either side of my eyes and sprayed more glitter in my hair. Dear reader, the thought of arriving at the wedding with face and hair "sparkling with glitter" horrified me. I was on a very tight schedule, and there just wasn't enough time to start all over again. Then Shanaz handed me the glitter.

"Dolley, is gift to you from Shanaz. Enjoy!"

Enjoy? I couldn't wait to see how much my husband, who was performing the wedding ceremony, would "enjoy" his glitter girl!

As I stepped out of the salon and into the bright California sunshine, a young family stopped in their tracks, stared, consulted each other, and said, "We sure like your sparkles," as their preschooler circled me, his mouth wide open.

My husband is the strong, silent type and a full-blooded Swede. I call him my Viking. He is a man who thinks before he speaks, and so it wasn't until we were almost halfway home in the car that Tom said quietly, "Honey, is that glitter?"

"Ah, yes. Shanaz did it."

Silence ... Then ... "Honey, I really like it." Who knew? This middle-aged, conservative father of two, my husband of many years, liked the glitter! We went into the house, changed into nicer clothing, and then off to the wedding we went, glitter and all.

On the way my husband spoke words that I never would have expected from him: "Honey, I think most of the glitter came off when you were getting dressed. You may want to freshen it up a little." Oh my goodness, did my ears hear correctly? Would I like to "freshen" my glitter? I opened what I thought was glitter paste only to find out too late that it was really fine glitter *powder*. It flew all over the car, Tom, and me. The more we tried to brush it off, the more it went everywhere. Glitter stuck to our hands, our clothing, Tom's wedding ceremony notes and Bible, anything and everything it came in contact with. We arrived at the wedding, and people looked at us like, "Okay, and what do we have here?" I actually heard some out-of-town guests whisper, "California ... that's California for you."

Tom just shimmered, sparkled, and glowed as he stood before the bride and groom at the front of the church. Actually, my heart skipped a beat as I looked at my beloved Viking who had now become my knight in shining armor too.

Later, at the reception, guests quickly addressed what was so obvious: "We just love your glitter." To which I responded, "Would you like some?" And surprisingly they all said, "Yes." Glitter was passed back and forth and returned to me. Then a frail little grandma at the far end of the table said, "I want some too." During the "glittering," my husband visited with other guests and returned with special requests from several tables for ... *glitter*. We all had so much fun, and a wedding never shimmered, glimmered, and sparkled with so much joy. Which, believe it or not, brings me to the point: Don't miss the joy.

Sometimes we get so stuck in the ordinary that we miss the extraordinary ... joy. Thankfully there wasn't enough time to wash my face and hair that day. I think the Lord led me to that time frame in order to see, hear, feel, and share joy. In this case, joy was the unexpected shimmer of gold glitter. And it created a golden bridge of communication and blessing between strangers as they celebrated the marriage of a young couple. How many other joys do you and I miss every day because of reservation or what we consider to be "good taste," and how many opportunities do we miss to bring a little joy to the hearts of others?

Would you like some glitter?

Dolley Carlson (California) is the author of the *Gifts from the Heart* book series. As a frequent speaker, she shares hope and joy with women across America and around the globe. Dolley and her husband live in California and have two grown daughters.

"Risky Living"

BY KAREN HEARL

"Mom, guess what. Our band has been asked to play for GMA week in Nashville. Why don't you come down." My single musician son had just invited me to a major Christian rock event.

"C'mon, Mom, it will be fun." Reluctantly I agreed to this "out of my comfort zone" experience. *After all,* my reasoning-self intoned, *I'm over fifty and can afford to take some risks.* Fifteen bands, six rock concerts, and seven clubs later I realized it had been a great adventure. Furthermore, I discovered that I had made a significant transition in my life.

Risk. Some are born to "push the envelope." Not me. I liked a sure thing; stability, direction, goals, and safety were my anchors. Somehow, at this stage in my life, I was learning that it was okay to try new things without fear of failure. It was an amazing discovery to learn that I really enjoyed the music and the beat. I am now a regular attendee and promoter of Christian bands in concert and on CD.

"How will you ever know unless you try?" my mother used to challenge me. And then she would add, "Always do your best." I couldn't reconcile the two ends of the spectrum; excellence and risk taking.

After 50, my husband and I moved from coast to coast. During that period of change and leaving the familiar, I found myself in an aimless maze. My husband continued his pastorate in a new location. The loss of job, position, and close friendships was devastating. We left behind our children and our first grandchild. Even though I tried to engage in my new environment, I was miserable. Life begins at fifty? My empty nest became a tomb without hope for the future. It took several months to make my definite choice. I determined not to live in a birdcage with futility or without a sweet song.

Intellectually and spiritually I knew that God had led us to this place of ministry. I had balked at even praying for God's will when the opportunity came. My faulty reasoning affected my husband's deep desire to be God's servant. Finally, I prayed a halfhearted prayer of submission, "Lord, please make me willing to be willing." And He did. However, I was still keeping my comfort closet locked.

Over the years since that invitation to Nashville, God has brought many new challenges, risk-taking situations, and pioneering opportunities to my doorstep. I have been reminded again of God's great grace and love as He led Sarah, Deborah, Ruth, Esther, and Priscilla into uncertain, faith-building scenarios. I needed to be shaken loose, freed up to step out in faith, and challenged to try new things that would bring people to the foot of the Cross.

This second half of life is better than the first. I am free to be. Life has new meaning. Isaiah 43:18–21 reminds us not to play old tapes in our heads. God is doing a "new" thing. We are called to anticipate and rejoice as the "streams come to the desert." My desert experience cleared my head and healed my heart; I became thirsty for those things that count for the kingdom. I am no longer satisfied with "safe" things that are just adequate. I do want God's very best. He has made "streams and rivers" of great blessing in my desert. In addition to new opportunities for ministry, there have been vibrant, life-giving, and energizing relationships. My learning curve on the subject of God's great grace has skyrocketed. Life is full of joy-filled, unexpected, and welcome surprises.

Elsie G. came into my life when we moved to New England. I was drawn to her by her sparkle and her "living on the edge" dynamic. She is more than seventy years of age. Nothing stops her. Every year she volunteers for a short-term mission trip from the Czech Republic to Mongolia to the highlands of Peru. Her job description includes everything from chief-cook-and-bottle-washer to teaching Vacation Bible School to street witnessing. And then there is Nell. Now in her middle eighties and widowed for the second time, she conducts Bible classes in her home and reaches out to mentor new believers. Elsie J. is ninety-four, and nothing stops her. She is responsible for the transportation and special needs of her ninety-plus friends. These women are encouragers. They bring zest to life and witness for Jesus. I am learning valuable life lessons from them—these over-fifty "girlfriends."

By the way, if you see a slightly overweight middle-aged woman in a red jacket and jeans clapping with the beat, jumping up and down, and waving at her son on stage in the stadium under the glare of the lights, that's me. And … I am enjoying every minute of the journey!

Karen Hearl (California), a Bible teacher and retreat speaker, has a heart's desire to encourage women in their walk with Jesus Christ. A pastor's wife for forty years, she is involved in leadership training for denominational and regional ministries.

TRUTH SEVEN:

Perseverance Pays Off

"Perspective"

BY LUCINDA SECREST MCDOWELL

I have been traveling this earth a half-century now, and I thought nothing much could surprise me anymore. But I was wrong.

Recently I learned that twenty years ago a woman I never met prayed a desperate prayer three thousand miles away. Then she died.

What surprised me?

That I am the answer to that prayer.

It was a beautiful spring day when I arrived in Boston where I would be one of the seminar speakers for a large inspirational event. When the director informed me that the keynote speaker wanted to meet me, I was both puzzled and pleased. I had read this speaker's books, facilitated a class based on her video teaching, and heard her speak in other large venues. But I couldn't help wondering, *Why does she want some private time with me?*

After a busy morning, I was taken to the green room where I was introduced to this speaker, and we had tea and conversation together. We hit it off immediately, and I soon heard something that changed my whole life's perspective.

She began by telling me that many years ago she was speaking in Seattle, and someone asked her to visit the hospital and pray with a young woman who was dying of liver cancer. "Cindy, I want to tell you what your husband's late wife and I talked about just before she died."

I gulped. I wasn't sure I was ready for this. I had never met Inka, Mike's wife of ten years, but I knew her family, all of whom lived in Holland. And, of course, I had gone to court and adopted her three small children after she died. But, though I hate to admit it, I had spent my seventeen years of marriage feeling alternately threatened by her memory and grateful to her memory. Right then, all I felt was curious.

"It was hard," she continued. "Inka knew she was dying, and she told me so. And it was especially hard because she was so happy to finally have a baby girl to go along with her two little boys, and it saddened her to realize that she wouldn't be able to raise her children. She went on to say that she knew that Mike would marry again, and she wanted him to do so. But then she broke down and confessed that she was so troubled in her spirit because, while she suspected her four-year-old son and one-year-old daughter would be fine, she was so worried about the future of her six-year-old son, born with mental retardation.

"Through her tears Inka cried, 'I just know there will never be a woman who can love him and help him with all his many special needs.'"

The speaker, who was holding my hands now as tears ran down my cheeks, continued. "Cindy, I prayed with her then and there, and we prayed with power, asking God to give her peace, and to provide for the husband and three precious children she would leave behind. We prayed that through God's grace, He would send a mother who could love and nurture the special needs of each of her children. And we prayed for that woman, whoever she might be, that God would give her all she needed for the great task at hand.

"After we prayed I looked at Inka's face, and it was full of peace as she told me, 'I know God has answered this prayer, and I can now release them all to Him.' I left the hospital room that day knowing that our precious Lord was comforting His own and providing for her in His way and His time. And I vowed I would continue to pray for the woman who would mother Mike and Inka's children. And I have."

By this time I was openly crying as she turned to me and said in the most gentle way and yet with great conviction, "Cindy, you are the answer to that prayer. I have prayed for you for twenty years, and I wanted to meet you and tell you in person of God's great moving in your life and in the lives of your family."

I am the answer to that prayer.

It's one thing to know the *facts* of a situation: I knew I married a widower. I knew I adopted his three small children who had no memory of their first mother. I knew our oldest son had terrific needs as a child, and that all the kids, while blessed with a great father, had been without a mom during three formative years before we married. It's quite another thing to learn the *heart* of a situation: the confidences between two women and the desires and concerns of a dying young mother.

That day as I sat alone in the little room, trying to sort out my feelings, I thought back to the years of raising my four children. (We had another daughter five years after the adoption.) The early years of our marriage had been so difficult, and I had faltered at times wanting so desperately to be what each one needed and yet feeling so lacking. At times I thought that all I had going for me was the deep *desire* to be the kind of mother whose love could transform and teach and heal.

But my love could not do those things.

Only God's love can transform. Only God's wisdom can teach. And only God's grace can heal.

But, remarkably enough, He did it in *partnership* with me. I was merely the vessel, willing to be an answer to someone else's prayer, all the while finding answers to my own prayers for a loving family: "He who calls you is faithful, and he will do it" (1 Thess. 5:24 RSV).

Today is the twenty-second anniversary of the day Inka entered into glory, leaving her husband and children behind. Soon Mike and I and the four kids will gather from around the country for a special family time: Tim graduated from college five years ago and currently works in Seattle. The "baby," Fiona, graduated from university two years ago and works in Washington, D.C. Our fourth child, Maggie, is in high school—she keeps us young. And what of that special-needs son, the one whom Inka prayed for so diligently? Well, Justin is now twenty-nine and has worked in the same restaurant for almost eight years. Living in his own apartment, he is active in Bible study and has won several gold medals in the International Special Olympics.

Does God answer prayer? Of course.

Is He finished with me or my husband or our children? Of course not.

We all continue to struggle and search and stumble and soar, but in the midst of the journey we are convinced that we are guided and protected by the One who knows our every need and heals our deepest pain. One who calls us to persevere.

I am grateful for this glimpse into God's faithfulness. Much of the time we see answers only when we reach eternity and everything is fully revealed. But I think God sent this speaker my way to give me an extra dose of encouragement and perseverance as I face the fresh needs of my now-grown children. The bottom line is this: *are we willing to be an answer to someone else's prayers?* If we are, then, should God choose to use us, He will guide us and provide for us everything we need: "For this God is our God for ever and ever; he will be our guide even to the end" (Ps. 48:14).

Lucinda Secrest McDowell, M.T.S. (Connecticut) presents "Encouraging Words that Transform" through her international conference speaking and writing. A graduate of Gordon-Conwell Seminary, she is the author of five books including *Quilts from Heaven, Women's Spiritual Passages,* and *Amazed by Grace.* www.EncouragingWords.net

"Hope Has Its Reasons"

BY REBECCA MANLEY PIPPERT

One thing is clear from Christian testimonies. Different things change for different people at different times and in different ways. Some people meet God and change dramatically. They are so transformed that we can hardly believe the difference when we see them. Others experience change more like a refinement that takes place slowly over time. Only God knows the reasons why it is so, and to pretend otherwise is presumptuous and cruel.

But what of situations where there seems to be no change at all, and we are completely in the dark? What kind of realistic hope are we to hold to? There are three things I have found helpful in facing that question. First, there is the question of our **basic expectations**. Second, there is the question of **our part**. Third, there is the question of **God's part**—or more accurately, our response to having no idea what God's part is. How are we to trust when we are completely in the dark? What faith needs is what Os Guiness calls "suspended judgment." This principle means that we may be in the dark about some situations, but we are not in the dark about God.

Christians are people of hope and not despair. Because we know that God, who had the first word, will have the last. He is never thwarted or caught napping by the circumstances of our lives. To have faith in Jesus does not mean we try to pretend that bad things are really good. Rather we know that God will take our difficulties and weave them into purposes we cannot see as yet. And when He is done, the day will be more glorious for our having gone through the difficulties. We are not unmindful of the difference between what is evil and what is good. We know that if the logic of His love nailed Jesus to the cross, we have no right to go another way.

But our lives can be lived well, with courage and joy, because we live by the hope of the resurrection. So no matter what life lands in our laps, if we will only trust God and wait, and never lose heart, the song we sing one day will be of victory. And then, with battles over, the time will come when faith becomes sight and hope fulfillment, and our whole beings are united with the God we love. Joy of all joys, goal of our desire, all that we long for will be ours for we will be His.

For the moment, though, we are still on the road. The gap between promise and performance is still the tension of our faith. Yet hope in Christ is the most compelling incentive in the world. Hope has its reasons after all.

Rebecca Manley Pippert (Kentucky) is an internationally acclaimed speaker and best-selling author of *Out of the Saltshaker, Hope Has Its Reasons,* and *A Heart Like His.* Her new teaching and training ministry is Salt Shaker Ministries. www.SaltShaker.org

"Keep Climbing"

BY DIANE M. KOMP

Some years ago in the clouds above a 700-year-old baroque Austrian town, I beheld an alpine apparition of health and vigor. That day I had planned to treat myself to a panoramic view of Innsbruck, but before I could enjoy the view I had to puff my way uphill to a cable car that would speed me to the top. On the path behind me I heard the brisk footfall of a seasoned hiker. This power-walker possessed far more wind for the work than I did that day.

"Grufs Gott" ("God's Greeting!") called an elderly woman in folklore dress. In almost comic contrast to her silver-braided hair, lace-trimmed blouse, green-print dirndl, and cranberry apron were her mud-brown boots, khaki wool socks, and enormous calf muscles. Thick veins coursed over her gastrocs like Popeye's spinach-fed biceps. Those robust legs had known a lifetime of marching up that mountain, over eighty years' worth, I reckoned by her wrinkled, smiling face.

It wasn't long before this vision of elderly fitness disappeared from my view. Later, as my cable car lazily ascended up to the Hungerberg station, I caught sight of her again through the clouds, charging up by foot toward the 2,800-foot plateau. The luminescence of her righteous sweat put me to shame. But that old doll in a dirndl had an inner glow of happiness and contentment, the sort of conviction that she would live to be one hundred and love every minute of it.

Why did such a charming sight as Heidi—I had to give her a name in my book of memories—exhaust me? A younger woman of forty-five at the time, I considered packing my hiking boots and heading home to vegetate in front of a fireplace. I even wondered whether I wanted to live into my eighties, much less survive to be a hundred. There are days in my life when I'm not sure that I'll make it through to supper! But Heidi is just the type of company I need in the clouds that surround me. I need friends who can show me how the power of God can sustain me all the days of my life.

Heidi would be almost a hundred years old today. I'll look for her on that mountain the next time I visit Innsbruck. Somehow I know that this spirited old woman in hiking boots is still glowing and growing today as she approaches her centennial mark. And somehow I know that even on the days that Heidi chooses a solitary walk up her beloved mountains, she will never be alone.

Heidi reminds me of a word that the psalmist uses to describe God and His love: steadfast. When you're tired and don't want to go on, steadfast sounds like intimidation. But when God attends our path, steadfast is just the gift we want—the strength to go on.

Diane M. Komp (Connecticut) was a professor of pediatric oncology at Yale University and has authored several books including *Images of Grace, Anatomy of a Lie,* and *Why Me? A Doctor Looks at the Book of Job.*

"Time Will Tell"

BY LORIE WALLACE BARNES

Almost half-century has now passed for me, and I wonder: *Where has the time gone?* Solomon wrote, "There is a time for everything, and a season for every activity under heaven: a time to be born and a time to die" (Eccl. 3:1–2). Time is so important to us all. Many of my friends and their children have electronic Palm Pilots to plan their days, while I am always reaching for my old calendar. We even have the Atomic Clock here in Boulder, Colorado, which serves as one of the standards by which the world tells time.

When I served as the director of Promise Preschool, my wonderful staff of four teachers and I met each month to discuss our little preschool's upcoming time schedule for the holidays. There was Dad's Night, the Thanksgiving Feast, Christmas family chapels, and of course, the Christmas parties. At one particular meeting, we paused as we launched into the holidays to reflect on the "fruits of the Spirit" as found in Galatians 5:22–23. I had written each "fruit of the Spirit" on a slip of paper, and we put all of them into a jar to serve as a reminder for us during the holidays. Each of us drew out a different "fruit" from the jar. I happened to choose "self-control," which was timely, as most of the leftover Halloween candy had become treats for me. My friend and colleague, Cathy, chose "faithfulness." Another teacher chose "patience," and yet another selected "gentleness." Little did we know that day how our friend Cathy's faith and ours would be challenged so soon. But God certainly knew.

By Thanksgiving, Cathy was experiencing dizzy spells, and felt so ill that her family's plans to visit her grandmother were cancelled. Cathy did not come back to the preschool after the Thanksgiving break, because she was not feeling any better. After a CAT scan revealed there was a tumor at the base of her brain, she had immediate surgery. This was when our staff and students learned that "Miss Cathy" was very ill and that her prognosis was grim.

Time stood still as the reality of Cathy's illness stunned us all. The moms gathered to pray, the children gathered to pray, casseroles were planned, and baby-sitting was set up for Cathy's little children. We learned that the cancer was so aggressive that Cathy's remaining time on earth was quite short. Cathy would never see her fiftieth birthday.

Time. A point in history. A point on the timeline. God came to meet us through His Son Jesus Christ, and it was an event that split history in two. Because of Jesus' birth, and because of His death and resurrection, my friend's faith in Him placed her in the presence of God's glory forever.

Ireneaus, the second-century theologian, once said, "The glory of God is a person fully alive." Cathy had lived her life to the fullest. Philip Yancey has written, "The life you clutch, hoard, guard and play safe with is in the end a life worth little to anybody, including yourself, and only a life given away for love's sake is a life worth living." Cathy's life was marked by the way in which she had given her life away to the Lord long before she battled cancer, and the love of God was very evident in her life as a result of her abandonment to Christ her Lord.

This death served as a wake-up call for me personally. I have often wondered how I would answer Saint Peter at the pearly gates if he asked me, point blank, "So, Lorie, what did you do with your time on earth?" I could say, "Well, I watched for the Foley's Red Apple Sale at the local department store, I watched my weight (go up and down several times), I did lots of laundry, and I cleaned more than a thousand bathrooms in my lifetime." However, I must be honest and ask myself: "How many people have learned about the hope that lies within me?" (see 1 Peter 3:15).

Tony Campolo recently said at a youth conference held here in Colorado, "People come to Boulder to find themselves, but what people need to realize is that, as Jesus said, you only find yourself when you lose yourself." My question is: "Will I make the center of history—Jesus Christ—the center of my next hour, my next day, my next fifty years?" Isn't it true that we feel we are most alive when we have given up our agendas and laid down our lives so that others may know Him?

I know my friend Cathy is in heaven. The question each of us must ask ourselves is: "What am I doing with the time I have here on earth before I join all the other saints who have gone before me?"

Lorie Wallace Barnes (Colorado), a graduate of Gordon-Conwell Seminary, is a freelance writer for Group Publishing. When she's not working or speaking at retreats, she's out running a marathon, hiking, or drinking latte with friends and family.

"Investing in What Will Last"

BY LAEL ARRINGTON

When my only child was in school and I was nearing forty, I remember thinking, *What have I* done *in my life?* It was a great impetus for me to think about priorities and strategy and what I wanted to exchange my life for. Physically limited in my options due to rheumatoid arthritis, I turned back to my gifts—an ability to see the big picture, a passion for proclaiming God's truth boldly, and a goodly share of creativity. "Please God," I begged, "use me. Use these gifts and talents You've given me *for the kingdom.*" I thought about how people and God's Word are the two things that will go with us from this life to the next. "Help me to invest in what will last."

On the homefront I was trying to guard my commitment to my husband and son and, although it has never been my strongest suit, be the caregiver for them God wanted me to be. I wish I had done it with more delight from the beginning, but God can take inordinate amounts of resignation and duty and bring forth a good harvest, even creating a heart of greater delight along the way.

Now, twelve years later, I am enjoying the dividends of my decisions to invest my time and gifts in things that will really last by caring for my family and studying, teaching, and writing. I love sharing God's Truth, telling stories, and encouraging my audience and readers to look at the big picture, living with the prophet Jeremiah's "big question" mentally taped on back of our eyelids, "What will [we] do in the end?" (Jer. 5:31). Investing in the world's ethic of youth, beauty, and power means sinking everything into depreciating assets.

Speaking of depreciating assets, even though I can't see as well as I used to, I can still look in the mirror and verify the truth of King Solomon's statement that time and chance happen to us all (see Eccl. 9:11). Oh, how the mighty high school beauty queen has fallen! (see 2 Sam. 1:19). And I don't just mean wrinkles, pooches, and too much gray. My hands are crippled; my tendons are broken. But that's why God made voice-recognition software. When it got to the point last spring that I almost couldn't walk much less stand and deliver a message, God used a wonderful orthopedic surgeon and much prayer and support from our church family to give me more mobility than I have had in years on my new bionic knee.

Sowing years of commitment to my family has reaped its own rewards. God has blessed my husband and his ministry in tangible ways. When I took some old friends who live out of town through our church recently, I was reminded again how much our church family has grown and expanded. Together my husband, Jack, and I are a team for the kingdom, accomplishing far more together than we ever could individually. We enjoy our empty nest because it is a home base for ministry in peoples' lives.

Walking with our young adult son through his struggles with God has taught me that not all of the harvest we have sown ripens into nice predictable fruit. As I pour out my heart to the Lord for him I also plead, "Lord, help me not to demand seeable results." The perseverance I have learned through twenty-three years of rheumatoid arthritis and many years of ministry is helping me to wait to see what God is growing in my son's life. More than anything, my hurt over our son has shown me the lavishness of God's grace. Yes, He rewards my obedience, but He overlooks so much foolishness and failure. In the end, everything I have and am is grace. It's all sheer grace.

On my fiftieth birthday, I hardly looked up. There was no grand celebration. There wasn't time. I was pounding down the homestretch of a book deadline, doing what I absolutely *love* to do. *Afterwards* we celebrated. My friends presented me with the most awesome "Memory Book" at a lovely china and crystal luncheon. They had sent the pages of this specially crafted "work of heart" out to a long list of old friends, new friends, and author friends. Decorated with original writing, drawings, old photos and cartoons, the stories and tributes make me laugh and cry.

This book is a *priceless* treasure because I had already forgotten way too much of the things they wrote beside the words: "Remember when … " For me, birthdays are getting better and better because I am getting closer and closer to the greatest celebration of all. The really *big* returns on my daily decisions to invest wholeheartedly in a life lived for God's kingdom are yet to come. The most *fantastic* birthdays are still ahead. Because of God's *Amazing Grace,* we will have even *more* to celebrate …

> *When we've been there ten thousand years,*
> *Bright, shining as the sun,*
> *We've no less days to sing God's praise*
> *Than when we first begun.*

Lael Arrington (Texas) writes and speaks about the challenge to live for God's kingdom in today's culture. Author of *Worldproofing Your Kids* and *Pilgrim's Progress Today,* she has been featured in *Focus on the Family* and *World* magazines. www.LaelArrington.com

"One Day We Shall Dance!"

BY JONI EARECKSON TADA

Everywhere we go in Poland people give us flowers—fresh, thick bouquets of friesians and sweet pea, tulips and gladiola in full bloom in our drab hotel rooms.

But how odd it is to see these same flowers swishing in the wind. Here. Here in Auschwitz. Even though the grounds of this death camp are so very tidy, delicate wisps of wildflowers crop up here and there, around the bases of brick buildings and trunks of trees. We wonder if the government, which operates a museum here, has sown wildflower seeds to brighten this horrible, depressing place.

"What are you thinking?" my husband Ken asks, stooping to pluck a wildflower.

"I was thinking of Tante Corrie ... Corrie ten Boom," I finally answer. "She was in a place not unlike this." I nod toward the field of ghosts. "By all accounts she should have died forty years ago in that concentration camp," I sigh.

Ken shakes his head in wonder. "Who would have thought she would leave that awful place. At fifty years of age," he marvels, his eyes fastened on the crumbled incinerators just yards away. "And then to start a whole new ministry."

I recall Tante Corrie's recent funeral at a small suburban cemetery a few miles south of Los Angeles. It was the flowers that impressed me that day too. No hothouse blooms stuck in Styrofoam cut-out shapes of hearts or crosses or doves. No white satin banners with gold-sprinkled messages of sympathy. Instead, there were vases—tens of vases—of freshly cut tulips of yellow and red. Bouquets of dewy white carnations and bunches of heavy red roses someone had clipped from Corrie's backyard.

The casket was closed. The music was Bach. The eulogies were glowing but understated. The only extravagance was the profusion of flowers, and the little stone chapel was filled with a sweet fragrance.

Now I sit in silence in this vast field, memories of Corrie stirring my thoughts. The only things that move are the wind and the daisies. It is at once striking and poignant. For Corrie, who came out of the pit of this hell, would be the first to say that the suffering in this place confronted her with the reality of the love or hate in her own heart. The confinement of her lonely cell attacked her own vanity and lonely pride. The crushing needs of her fellow prisoners constantly exposed her own need to give and share. She could not blame. She could only forgive.

I drop my gaze to the daisies Ken has tucked into the straps of my arm splints. A knowing smile crosses my lips. I would be the first to say that my wheelchair confronts me daily with the love or hate in my own heart. It attacks my pride and constantly exposes my need to give to others who suffer. I have no one to blame for my circumstances.

I recall another memory of Corrie and flowers: the evening at that convention when, amid the applause of thousands, she lifted her bouquet of roses toward heaven. She would be the first to say that books on a best-seller list mean nothing—except that lives are changed through them. She would say that a first-run major motion picture of her life was not worth the accolades—except that people were helped through it. Even a ministry that took her all over the world with opportunities to speak and meet headlining names in evangelical circles—even that, she would say, only counts in the kingdom as far as it serves Christ.

And I would say the same. In both my public ministry and my private life with Ken, God constantly asks me to uncover my face. But that is my joyous choice: to ask Him to chasten and purify and melt any resistance to change I might secretly hold on to.

I smile. In fact, I throw my head back and laugh out loud. And I tell Ken of the time I first met that remarkable woman years ago when we were both attending a convention where our new books were being presented. Corrie approached from down the long red-carpeted hallway of a hotel. People were all about and many sought her attention. But she strode directly toward me, hiked her cane on her elbow, reached for my hand with those strong hands that all survivors have, and announced in her thick Dutch accent, "One day, my friend, we will be dancing together in heaven because of the Lord Jesus."

And today I can laugh and rejoice because Corrie is dancing now. Over the devil and over this place.

And once changed, we shall join her.

Joni Eareckson Tada (California) is founder and president of Joni and Friends. Her latest book is *The God I Love*. For more on her life and ministry see www.JoniandFriends.com

Permissions

"Become the Best Possible You" is adapted from *How to Live Right When Your Life Goes Wrong*. Copyright © 2003 by Leslie Vernick. Used by permission of WaterBrook Press, Colorado Springs, Colo. All rights reserved.

"Pursuing Authentic Dreams" is excerpted from *What Will I Do with the Rest of My Life?* by Brenda Poinsett, © 2000. Used by permission of NavPress—www.navpress.com. All rights reserved.

"God Is Here" is excerpted from "Good News About the Resurrection" by Carol Kent in *Today's Christian Woman* magazine, March/April 2002. © 2002 Carol Kent. Used with permission.

"At the Window Again" is reprinted by permission from *And Then We Had Teenagers* by Susan Alexander Yates, Baker Books, a division of Baker Book House Company, copyright © 2001. Used with permission.

"We Need Each Other" originally appeared in *Have We Really Come a Long Way?* by Ruth Senter © 1997. Used with permission.

"Learning to Be a Comforter-Friend" is from *In His Everlasting Arms* by Gail MacDonald. © 2000 by Gail MacDonald. Published by Servant Publications, P.O. Box 8617, Ann Arbor, Michigan 48107. Used with permission.

About the Author

Every word you give me is a miracle word—
how could I help but obey?
Break open your words, let the light shine out,
let ordinary people see the meaning.

Psalm 119:129–130 MSG

Lucinda Secrest McDowell, M.T.S., presents contagious joy and hope through her humorous and profound words of encouragement and challenge.

A respected international conference speaker and author who has written for fifty-plus different magazines and collaborated on more than a dozen books, she was the recipient of the Mt. Hermon "Writer of the Year" award.

In addition to *What We've Learned So Far*, she has also authored *Amazed By Grace, Women's Spiritual Passages, Quilts from Heaven,* and *A Southern-Style Christmas.*

Active in the Advanced Writers & Speakers Association (AWSA), Cindy holds degrees from Gordon-Conwell Theological Seminary, Furman University, and studied at Wheaton Graduate School of Communication. Her professional experience includes editorial and communications staff for both "Thailand '80" and "Amsterdam '83" international conferences; missions, pastoral care, and women's ministry staff at large churches in both California and Connecticut; and radio producer and broadcaster.

An avid collector of quilts, pansies, stationery, teapots, and friends, Cindy currently makes her home in New England. She is married to the Reverend Michael McDowell and is the mother of two sons and two daughters.

My mission is to glorify God and live in His grace
and freedom,
and through the power of the Holy Spirit
to use my gifts to communicate God's faithfulness,
extend His grace, and encourage others to trust
Him fully.

L.S.M. 1993

To communicate with the author or to request information about her books and speaking engagements, please contact her at:

Mailing Address: Encouraging Words that Transform!
P.O. Box 290707
Wethersfield CT 06129 USA

Web site: www.EncouragingWords.net
Phone: (860) 257-WORD
Email: cindy@encouragingwords.net

Readers' Guide

For Personal Reflection or Group Discussion

BY LUCINDA SECREST McDOWELL

Readers' Guide

What have you learned so far in your journey of life? Has reaching middle age prompted you to ask some important questions and reflect on where you've been and how you will live for the time you have left?

What We've Learned So Far has offered stories by many fifty-plus women who affirm the seven important truths presented in each section of this book: Who I Am Is More Important Than What I Do, God Is in Control, Relationships Are to Be Celebrated, Freedom Is Found in Simplicity, Pain Either Destroys or Transforms, Life Is Full of Surprises, and Perseverance Pays Off.

Now it's your turn to examine each of these truths and come up with your own lessons and guidelines for living. These questions have been designed for use by individuals or by groups. You may also use this guide during personal devotions or in a small group book study.

However you utilize this study, my prayer is that it will bring you closer to your heavenly Father who still has wonderful things in store for your life, no matter your age!

TRUTH ONE: WHO I AM IS MORE IMPORTANT THAN WHAT I DO

1. Cindy ("Striving No More") described an identity crisis she experienced when first becoming a wife and mother of three. Have you ever had a similar wake-up call when your status or environment changed radically? How did you handle the insecurity and uncertainty?

2. What do you think was the most important lesson Karen ("What I'm Made For") learned? Has God ever gotten your attention through a similar faux pas?

3. Have you ever felt like the people Leslie ("Becoming the Best Possible You") mentioned who know all about spiritual life in their heads but not how to live it in their hearts? If you were to "stop trying and start training" what would that look like?

4. Anne ("Turning Things Around") realizes that "too often the expectations of *doing* crowd out the expectations we have of ourselves for *being*." Have you discovered the truth of God's grace—being a gift we don't deserve, "not of our own doing" (see Ephesians 2:8)? How?

5. Brenda ("Pursuing Authentic Dreams") shares that she spent many years avoiding her desires to write and speak because she felt

she didn't have choices. Do you desire to use your God-given abilities to risk something new and different at this time of life? Determine one tangible goal for pursuing that dream.

6. With which of Sharon's ("Going through Changes") five secrets of life at fifty do you most identify today? Why?

TRUTH TWO: GOD IS IN CONTROL

1. Like Cindy ("Out of Control") do you consider yourself a "control freak?" Can you remember times in your life when you were under someone else's control and vowed you would never be in that place again? How has this made it harder to relinquish your control to God?

2. In the middle of Carol's ("God Is Here") worst nightmare she discovered four evidences of the God of Hope being in control: Authentic Joy, A Faithful Companion, Power to Overcome, and Freedom from Fear. Which do you most need right now in your own experience of being out of control? Pray that God will make Himself real to you in this way.

3. Susan ("At the Window Again") shares the struggle of every mother and grandmother—letting go. She gives a litany of thanks to

God for His faithfulness in this season of life. Write your own Thankful List.

4. Have you ever lost your joy as Mary ("I Don't Want to Learn *That*") did during a time of emotional and physical upheaval? When she was slowly becoming spiritually numb, God spoke to her through the testimony of someone willing to embrace the crucified life (Elisabeth Elliot's *These Strange Ashes*). Do you have a similar message of hope, that came to you through a book, Scripture, or an encounter?

5. Peg ("Look Out Below") shares a time when God closed one door but opened a window to a new and better situation. He even provided financially in miraculous ways! Think of an "impossible" obstacle in your life right now. Pray that God will work a miracle and that you will have the wisdom to recognize His hand and follow with obedience.

6. Missionary Sarah ("Getting Older, Getting Better") had to do a lot of waiting on God to answer her prayers for a flight out of the jungle. Think of a time when you had to wait patiently on God. How did you handle it? How did you grow in the process?

TRUTH THREE: RELATIONSHIPS ARE TO BE CELEBRATED

1. Cindy ("Just Show Up") was greatly ministered to when her friend Maggie sat with her in the surgery waiting room. Think of a time when someone has shown up for you. How did it change your experience? Now think of a situation in which you could be the one to "just show up." Okay, do it!

2. Ruth ("We Need Each Other") never forgot that Mother Teresa ate in the basement with her fellow sisters rather than at the head table. What is one specific action you could take this week to show your friend how important she is to you?

3. Gail ("Learning to Be a Comforter-Friend") suggests that we offer our presence to others in the midst of their pain. Can you remember a time when a friend was suffering and you didn't know what to do or say? What did you do? How would you handle it differently now?

4. Cheri ("Praying Together") and her husband began praying together during a time of marital crisis, and it brought them closer to one another. Do you regularly pray with your husband? If he's open to the idea, why not initiate a weekly time together to simply share the people and concerns on your hearts. Then watch God work.

5. Anne ("Blessed to Be a Blessing") gives a great suggestion for honoring others by presenting Bible promises at a celebration. What do you think this gift meant to the young engaged couple? Next time you host a shower, farewell, birthday, or retirement party invite your guests to bring Scripture gifts and see how God blesses.

6. Maggie's ("Resident Alien") exploration of her family roots gave her both insight and inspiration for her own life. Do you know the story of your own grandmother or great-grandmother? Share this with your small group. Why not do some research and ask your relatives to share stories of her? And don't forget to pass them along as a legacy to the rest of the family.

7. If you, like Diane ("The Value of Family"), grew up in a Christian home, write down the most important spiritual lessons you learned from your parents. What do you think your own children would write if asked this same question?

TRUTH FOUR: FREEDOM IS FOUND IN SIMPLICITY

1. Have you ever felt like the collapsed clothes in Cindy's ("Too Much") closet? How did you climb out from under the burden of too busy or too much? What helped?

2. Martha ("The Second Half of the Ride") observes that many of us just "coast" during this season of life. What will you do today to intentionally embrace your second half?

3. Jeanne ("Simple Joy") offers five disciplines of simplicity: save up, free up, use up, fix up, and look up. Which of these is the hardest for you and what can you do to master it?

4. Have you, like Fran ("Simply Go Lightly"), lugged around an overstuffed spiritual suitcase? Name each item you want to empty at the feet of Jesus in order for your load to be lighter.

5. Mary ("Simplicity") quotes, "Someday, the things we own may end up owning us." Have you ever discovered this to be true? Name one situation where this is a danger and brainstorm about how you can make necessary changes.

TRUTH FIVE: PAIN EITHER DESTROYS OR TRANSFORMS

1. Patsy ("Mending Broken Hearts") encourages the hurting to sit down, weep, mourn, fast, and pray as a response to what God is doing in their lives. Think of an area of brokenness in your own life and walk through this exercise towards healing.

2. Judy ("Perfect Peace for Parents of Prodigals") learned an important lesson the day she turned fifty. What was it? How could this help you with a prodigal in your own life?

3. Ruth ("Running Partners") shares metaphorically about how God enabled her to run even when she felt crippled by the pain and rejection of divorce. Do you know beyond the shadow of a doubt that Jesus is present with you during the hardest parts of life's journey? How does that transform your outlook?

4. Like Lynne ("Learning Not to Walk") many of us struggle with physical loss, limitations, or pain at this season of life. How can you be both honest about your losses in life while also focusing on thankfulness for the daily blessings you have received?

5. Patricia ("Lost Years") survived a bout of mental illness in her deep depression. How did God meet her there? What did her own response do to change her life as a result of this experience?

6. Carole ("Transforming Losses") lost both her daughter and mother within a short time. What lessons had she learned from them (and also her sick husband), which helped her to be transformed instead of destroyed?

TRUTH SIX: LIFE IS FULL OF SURPRISES

1. Cindy ("Controlled Burning") struggled between the sight she saw and the father she trusted. When have you been tempted to question God as you observed devastating circumstances? How did He prove His faithfulness?

2. Did you live through the Jesus Movement like Linda ("I Never Dreamed It Would Be This Way")? When were you surprised to discover that being an "older woman" could be a good thing? How have you experienced that Jesus is enough?

3. What were Marta's ("Seeds of Summer") biggest surprises as the fiftyish mother of two toddlers? How did living in the African culture help her determine the two pillars of her identity?

4. Are you willing, like Virelle ("Have I Got What It Takes to Start Over?"), to uproot and begin fresh in a new place? What is the hardest part about this kind of change at our season of life?

5. Louise ("Grit and Glory") was haunted by questions of whether or not she had missed God's will for her life. Have you ever been tempted with the "should haves" and "if onlys" of life? How has Louise seen God working through her pain and special-needs son?

How do you think God can work through the path you have taken in life?

6. Is there something (even something good) that you need to give up in order to pursue a new path God has for you? How did this spur Cynthia ("The Day the Piano Moved Out") to pursue her doctorate in her fifties?

7. Dolley ("Shimmer, Glimmer, Sparkle, Joy") wore glitter to a wedding as a symbol of new joy. What can you add to your life, your personality, or your wardrobe to emphasize that God's joy is fresh every day?

TRUTH SEVEN: PERSEVERANCE PAYS OFF

1. How do you think Cindy ("Perspective") felt when the speaker told her the story of her long ago visit with a dying mother? How did God answer both Inka's and Cindy's prayers? Are you willing to be the answer to someone else's prayer?

2. Becky ("Hope Has Its Reasons") says, "Christians are people of hope and not despair." What does she mean by that? Do you find a gap between promise and performance? How can you live with "suspended judgment?"

3. Lorie ("Time Will Tell") asks the question "What am I doing with the time I have here on earth?" How would you answer that question? As you evaluate your own time priorities, what are some areas you'd like to change?

4. Lael ("Investing in What Will Last") is a prolific writer with crippled hands. Does that seem like a contradiction in terms? How can God use you to do the really important things, even with your limitations? Are you willing to persevere to make that happen?

5. Joni ("One Day We Shall Dance") admits that living in a wheelchair daily confronts her with the love or hate in her own heart. What has she discovered really matters in life? What did Corrie ten Boom say to her, and why is this an important promise for us all to remember?

Breath Prayers for Women - Take a Break for Time with God

Breath Prayers for Women

In our hurry-up-and-go lifestyle, many people today feel like they have very little time t o spend with God. Breath Prayers for Women is a wonderful book filled with heartfelt prayers that can help readers spend their days with enjoying God's company and surrounding their loved ones with prayer without giving up their "to-do" lists. Terrific for the woman on the go!
ISBN: 1-56292-254-8   ITEM #: 103679
5-1/2 x 8-1/2 PB 448P

The Mitford Series

Jan Karon

Follow the adventures of Father Tim in this delightful series about a town in the Blue Ridge Mountains.
5-1/2 x 8-1/2 PB

At Home in Mitford

Father Tim finds himself running on empty. A huge black dog adopts him, and a hostile mountain boy is thrust into his care. To add to his difficulties, a growing relationship with Cynthia Coopersmith, his new neighbor, stirs emotions he hasn't felt in years.
ISBN: 0-74592-629-0 ITEM #: 58909
448P

A Light in the Window

Cynthia has won Father Tim's heart, but he is afraid of letting go. Then a wealthy and powerful widow pursues him with cobbler and old sherry! The antidote to his dilemma rests in the history of his oldest and dearest parishioners and the family she didn't know she had.
ISBN: 0-74592-803-X ITEM #: 58917
416P

These High Green Hills

Father Tim fulfills Cynthia's conviction that deep down he is a man of romance, panache, and daring. Though his own cup of joy overflows, his heart goes out to those around him who so badly need healing.
ISBN: 0-74592-741-1 ITEM #: 58891
350P

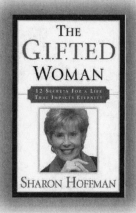

The G.I.F.T.ed Woman
12 Secrets for a Life that Impacts Eternity
Sharon Hoffman

Deep in the heart of women is a longing for true purpose and meaning in their lives, homes, and careers. And readers who have been experiencing this longing are not experiencing it by accident. In fact, women can learn to make life count more than ever with the help of speaker and author Sharon Hoffman. Her book reveals that God has placed unique gifts within women that can change their lives and the lives of others,

Hoffman's warm and personal style will inspire readers to grasp and live out their divine calling to be a G.I.F.T.ed woman--a Godly Influencer For Today!

ISBN: 0-78144-065-3 ITEM #: 103319
5-1/2 x 8-1/2 PB 224P

CROSSINGS®
THE BOOK CLUB FOR TODAY'S CHRISTIAN FAMILY

A Letter to Our Readers

Dear Reader:

In order that we might better contribute to your reading enjoyment, we would appreciate your taking a few minutes to respond to the following questions. When completed, please return to the following:

Andrea Doering, Editor-in-Chief
Crossings Book Club
401 Franklin Avenue, Garden City, NY 11530

You can post your review online! Go to www.crossings.com and rate this book.

Title _____ Author _____

1 Did you enjoy reading this book?

❑ Very much. I would like to see more books by this author!

❑ I really liked_____

❑ Moderately. I would have enjoyed it more if_____

2 What influenced your decision to purchase this book? Check all that apply.

❑ Cover
❑ Title
❑ Publicity
❑ Catalog description
❑ Friends
❑ Enjoyed other books by this author
❑ Other _____

3 Please check your age range:

❑ Under 18   ❑ 18-24
❑ 25-34   ❑ 35-45
❑ 46-55   ❑ Over 55

4 How many hours per week do you read? _____

5 How would you rate this book, on a scale from 1 (poor) to 5 (superior)?
_____

Name_____

Occupation_____

Address_____

City_____ State_____ Zip_____